Social Networking
for Business

Social Networking
for Business

Choosing the Right Tools and
Resources to Fit Your Needs

Rawn Shah

Vice President, Publisher: Tim Moore
Associate Publisher and Director of Marketing: Amy Neidlinger
Wharton Editor: Steve Kobrin
Editorial Assistant: Pamela Boland
Development Editor: Russ Hall
Operations Manager: Gina Kanouse
Senior Marketing Manager: Julie Phifer
Publicity Manager: Laura Czaja
Assistant Marketing Manager: Megan Colvin
Cover Designer: Alan Clements
Managing Editor: Kristy Hart
Project Editor: Lori Lyons
Copy Editor: Krista Hansing Editorial Services
Proofreader: Williams Woods Publishing Services, LLC
Indexer: Lisa Stumpf
Compositor: Jake McFarland
Manufacturing Buyer: Dan Uhrig

© 2010 by Pearson Education, Inc.
Publishing as Wharton School Publishing
Upper Saddle River, New Jersey 07458

Wharton School Publishing offers excellent discounts on this book when ordered in quantity for bulk purchases or special sales. For more information, please contact U.S. Corporate and Government Sales, 1-800-382-3419, corpsales@pearsontechgroup.com. For sales outside the U.S., please contact International Sales at international@pearson.com.

Company and product names mentioned herein are the trademarks or registered trademarks of their respective owners.

Printed in the United States of America

First Printing January 2010

ISBN-10 0-13-235779-8
ISBN-13 978-0-13-235779-1

Pearson Education LTD.
Pearson Education Australia PTY, Limited.
Pearson Education Singapore, Pte. Ltd.
Pearson Education North Asia, Ltd.
Pearson Education Canada, Ltd.
Pearson Educatión de Mexico, S.A. de C.V.
Pearson Education—Japan
Pearson Education Malaysia, Pte. Ltd.

Library of Congress Cataloging-in-Publication Data

Shah, Rawn.
   Social networking for business : choosing the right tools and resources to fit your needs / Rawn Shah. — 1st ed.
      p. cm.
   Includes index.
   ISBN 978-0-13-235779-1 (hardback : alk. paper) 1. Business enterprises—Computer networks. 2. Leadership. 3. Computer software—Development. I. Title.
   HD30.37.S44 2010
   658'.056754—dc22

                                                                                            2009035891

For the future social computing
world of my son Ryhan

Contents at a Glance

Contents

Acknowledgments

Rarely will you find a writer who has not undergone some degree of social discovery and validation of ideas, this book project not withstanding. I would like to thank the managers and mentors who have encouraged me to participate in activities that have resulted in this book: Greg Meyer, Laura Bennett, Tom Hartrick, Jim Coughlin, Scott Bosworth, Heather Huffman, and Laura Cappelletti on the IBM developerWorks team, and Gina Poole and Wolfgang Kulhanek on the Social Software Enablement team.

There are many others who have had an impact on this book: Jeanne Murray, Younghee Overly, Luis Suarez, Joshua Scribner, Peter Kim, Branavan Ganesan, PK Sridhar, Jeanette Fuccella, Jennette Banks, Candace York, Anne Beville, Will Morrison, David Sink, Rand Ries, Rachel Happe, Michael Muller, Joan Dimicco, Kate Ehrlich, Aaron Kim, Pam Nesbitt, Hardik Dave, Randy Atkins, David Singer, Bob Pulver, John Rooney, David Millen, John 'Boz' Handy-Bosma, Bill Johnston, Mohan Tanniru, the many friends in IBM's worldwide Social Software Ambassador community, and the ambient genius of the social media folks on Twitter.

I need to thank the enduring efforts of the team at Wharton School Press: Tim Moore, Russ Hall, Gina Kanouse, and Lori Lyons—who have helped bring this vision to reality. Additional thanks go to the pleasant, understanding staff at the Starbucks #5505 on University and Euclid that have seen me almost daily, sitting in the same chair quietly working away over the past three years. Finally, thanks to my wife and family for encouraging and helping while I worked on this book.

About the Author

Rawn Shah is best practices lead in the Social Software Enablement team in IBM Software Group, helping to bring the worldwide population of more than 350,000 IBMers closer together and to improve their productivity through social software. His job involves investigating the wide range of social computing technologies, collecting best practices, measuring the usage and behavior of social software as it impacts productivity, and advising on implementation, governance, and operations.

In his prior job as community program manager for IBM developerWorks, he led a team of operations and development staff covering the worldwide network of thousands of communities, blogs, wikis, and social computing environments supported by IBM. He also led the creation of the developerWorks spaces software tool, a multi-tenant system to allow individuals and teams to bring many social tools together into their own focused social environments.

An avid software gamer, he has been involved in the online gaming world since 1990, both as a player, a guild leader, and hosting massively multiplayer games. He has witnessed how these social environments have grown from underground curiosities to the billion-dollar businesses of today, with the nature of social grouping and collaboration evolving hand in hand with every new offering.

He has previously served as network administrator, systems programmer, Web project manager, entrepreneur, author, technology writer, and editor in different business environments: as a sole proprietor, in a small startup, and in a Fortune 50 company. He has contributed to six other books, the most recent being the category-leading *Service Oriented Architecture Compass*, which since has been translated into four languages. His nearly 300 article contributions to technical periodicals such as JavaWorld, LinuxWorld, CNN.com, SunWorld, Advanced Systems, and Windows NT World Japan, covered a wide range of topics from software development to network environments to consumer electronics.

In his spare time, he is a student and teacher of Ryuseiken Battodo, a Japanese art of sword fighting, helping middle school, high-school and college students, and adults to develop mental focus and physical agility.

1

Social Computing on the Ascent

Determining where to focus innovation efforts is a challenging open-ended and uphill battle. Most businesspeople look for answers from product and technical leadership balanced against the current business strategy. This often hinders a wider look at what needs and opportunities exist.

In large multinational organizations such as IBM, with many different product lines, research interests, and industry foci, this is multiplied. IBM's answer was simple: Ask everyone. In 2006, its InnovationJam online event drew 150,000 business partners, employees, and even family members to focus on a number of high-level innovation themes. IBM has conducted such InnovationJams since 2001, but this was by far the largest. Thousands of users brainstormed, discussed, and debated ideas within each theme online to improve how people stay healthy, work toward a better planet, and improve finance and commerce. By committing $100 million to build new businesses for each theme, IBM created smarter healthcare payment systems, real-time language services, and a 3D Internet project. Gathering input for innovation initiatives and corporate social responsibility isn't new, but IBM's approach was an innovation in itself for its time—the company cast a wide net and invited a multitude of perspectives, expertise areas, and deliberation to arrive at the best ideas.

IBM isn't the only company working with groups of users on complex, subjective business problems. In its drive to provide innovative customer support, Verizon, a leading wireless phone and communications carrier, encourages a core of tech-savvy customers to answer deep-level technical support questions for others at no cost.[1] The company is taking advantage of a known phenomenon of users' desire to help others as they themselves tinker on the systems. With the expertise of Lithium Technologies, a consultancy in Emeryville, California, Verizon is quickly learning how to shape its community toward the focused business goal of customer support.

Amazon.com, the well-known retailer of books and other products online, is discovering other ways to involve the collective energies of many individuals in helping it sell more. Through customer reviews, recommendations of similar products, and categorization of items based on how people really see products fitting together, Amazon is driving return-customer sales.

The list goes on: Best Buy is asking its workforce to predict future prices for its inventory of products. Disney reaches an increasingly online generation of children ages 6–11 with a safe online world of *Club Penguin* designed just for them. Busy executives—Jonathan Schwartz (CEO of Sun Microsystems), Bill Marriott (Chairman and CEO of Marriott International), Bob Lutz (Vice Chairman of General Motors), and David W. Hill, Yao Ying Jia, and Tomoyuki Takahashi (design executives at computer manufacturer Lenovo[2])—now communicate regularly through Internet blogs to customers, shareholders, and other industry watchers. Chacha.com provides fee-based services that enable mobile and online users to ask any question, which Chacha.com hands to its collections of experts to find and provide answers. Many businesses are now actively investigating how to harness the collaborative strength of their customers through online sites such as MySpace, Facebook, Second Life, and Twitter. Other businesses help their employees or business partners discover skilled resources, share expertise, or even develop new products and projects within their company.

---

[1] Steve Lohr, "Customer Service? Ask a Volunteer" *New York Times* (online edition), 25 April 2009. Accessible at www.nytimes.com/2009/04/26/business/26unbox.html?_r=2&ref=business.

[2] Jonathan Schwartz blogs at http://blogs.sun.com/jonathan/. Bob Lutz's *FastLane* blog is at http://fastlane.gmblogs.com/. Bill Marriot blogs at www.blogs.marriott.com/brands/. Hill, Yao, and Takahashi from Lenovo blog at *Design Matters*, at http://lenovoblogs.com/designmatters/. The Lenovo team's design work on the Thinkpad laptop computer is the subject of Steve Hamm's *The Race for Perfect* (New York: McGraw-Hill, 2008).

From internal innovation to customer support, and even to developing new business services, all these companies are finding different ways to structure groups of people to work on common goals to solve business problems. You have probably used these tools, or others have used them to try to reach you. Like it or not, you will need to understand how they work, how they impact your business, or even how to turn them to your financial advantage. However, these companies aren't "managing people" in the classic sense of task assignments, job roles, and team projects today. The approach they're taking falls into a new field of software- and group-assisted business processes called *social computing*. (See the sidebar "Social Networking, Social Media, Social Computing: What's the Difference?")

According to the 2006 *Global CEO Study* by the IBM Institute for Business Value,[3] CEOs expect that the top three primary sources of new ideas and innovation will come from business partners, general employees (other than internal research and development), and clients; 75% of CEOs agree that collaboration is a key influencer of innovation. A McKinsey report[4] describes it as follows:

> Although collaboration is at the heart of modern business processes, most companies are still in the dark about how to manage it...they do a poor job of shedding light on the largely invisible networks that help employees get things done across functional, hierarchical, and business unit boundaries.

By framing collaboration toward specific goals and methods instead of a large, amorphous concept, social computing helps develop and direct innovative development in an organization. At the same time, social computing is shaking up a fundamental aspect of business: how people communicate and work together to produce results. It has an impact on many areas of business and management: It changes team and organizational unit structures, who can participate in and influence business decisions, decision-making processes, and the business environment that encourages people to work together effectively.

---

[3] *Global CEO Study 2006*, IBM Institute for Business Value (2006). Accessible from www-935.ibm.com/services/us/gbs/bus/html/bcs_ceostudy2006.html.

[4] R. L. Cross, R. D. Martin, and L. M. Weiss, "Mapping the Value of Employee Collaboration," *The McKinsey Quarterly*, no. 3 (2006): 29–41.

Social Networking, Social Media, Social Computing: What's the Difference?

Generally, *computation* means applying a defined set of procedures to solve a particular problem. In *social computing*, people become part of the overall computation system by examining, analyzing, and addressing the issues. Problems well suited for social computing are often the same ones that are difficult or unfeasible to solve using only software analysis and formulaic calculations: They're problems that require ingenuity or associative thinking, relationships and trust between people, and subjective knowledge.

This is social in the sense that it relies on groups of people interacting in some way. Although many people interact simply to keep in touch with friends or for their own personal entertainment, we're interested in how social computing techniques apply to business relationships and interactions that lead to results.

The role of software in social computing is to support the way people can interact and to frame the steps for them to work on loosely defined problems. The software helps users communicate, keep track of their interactions and relationships, collectively make choices and decisions, and filter the business results within the vast tracts of content and messages that these interactions produce. Not all social-software applications support all types of social computation. And software is only one necessary tool. Social computing also depends on human factors, such as the tasks people perform, how they interact, and what encourages them to participate.

Social computing accelerates the key business element of collaboration. It incorporates different approaches to collaboration—supported by IT infrastructure, well-defined user experiences, and tasks formulated to different business areas—while considering the culture of how people interact and collaborate. *Social networking* is a popular term referring to all kinds of social software tools. It also refers specifically to how users build networks of relationships to explore their interests and activities with others. The difference between social networking and social computing will become more apparent in later chapters. *Social media,* another popular term, refers to the online content, or methods to create, share, or build on such content through social means. By definition, a *social environment* is a virtual place where the interactions between the people involved in social computing take place. It has no one particular shape or form; instead, think of it as the vessel wherein ideas and interactions mix together into a complex recipe. Successful social computing involves determining the right ingredients, recipe, and preparation techniques that deliver the expected result.

These changes require new ways of thinking about how people work together in an organization. More important, larger business and customer trends are impacting the nature of how modern enterprises operate that in turn reinforces the need to apply social computing to business management processes.

Reshaping the Way We Work

Two main trends are changing how we work: an increased pace of business across the globe, and the way users are taking to online environments. These trends are meeting at a nexus that blatantly pushes organizations to investigate and implement more social interaction and online collaboration through social environments.

The speed of business is calling for strategic improvements in business agility through faster innovation, exploration of new and emerging markets, and increased partnering activities. To keep pace, organizations are focusing their strategic IT assets to institute faster computer networks for an increasingly flexible, mobile, and distributed workforce, enabling them to communicate complex information within the organization and with partners and customers. Although e-mail and Web access to support communications have become common in most organizations, corporate users are looking for better ways to organize their enterprise data, manage their business relationships, communicate detailed content, and discover new information, customers, and the expertise to guide them. For companies with a distributed workforce, simply keeping track of who works in their organization and what time zone they're in becomes a time-consuming task in itself.

The other significant trend is a swirl of changing online user behavior. A new wave of employees who have been active online from a young age are now entering the workforce and exemplify these changes particularly well. These "digital natives" have grown up Internet aware, actively using online software, visiting Web sites, and connecting and developing relationships over the virtual world of the Internet. According to the Pew Internet and American Life Project, 75% of adults age 18–24 and 57% age 25–34 have a profile on a social network site.[5] Eighty percent say that being a networked worker improves their ability to do their job, and 73% indicate that it improves their ability to share ideas with coworkers.[6]

How these digital natives use computers is also resulting in an increasing reliance on *cloud computing:* an emerging IT system in which data and applications reside entirely online instead of on any single computer or device. In the United States, 69% of users are moving to Web-based tools to manage their e-mail, photos, and files.[7] They use the Internet to research information about products, organizations, and even other people to guide their decisions. Their information can now also move with them as they change jobs. Their focus has shifted from "What's on my computer?" to "What information do I have access to?"

In a world where computers are everywhere, from the massive supercomputer systems in the largest corporations to Internet-capable household appliances, it seems that *people* are taking back some of the power previously relinquished to faceless devices and organizations. The tools of this new order are social interaction and collaboration—ironically, facilitated by the same computers that previously locked us away into fixed processes, compartmentalized information, and isolated workspaces.

---

[5] Amanda Lenhart, *Adults and Social Network Websites,* Pew Internet and American Life Project, January 2009. Available online at www.pewinternet. org/~/media//Files/Reports/2009/ PIP_Adult_social_networking_data_memo_FINAL.pdf.pdf.

[6] Mary Madden and Sydney Jones, *Networked Workers,* The Pew Internet and American Life Project, September 2008. Available online at www.pewinternet. org/~/media//Files/Reports/2008/PIP_Networked_Workers_FINAL.pdf.pdf.

[7] John B Horrigan, *Use of Cloud Computing Applications and Services,* Pew Internet and American Life Project, September 2008. Available online at www.pewinternet.org/~/media//Files/Reports/2008/PIP_Cloud.Memo.pdf. pdf.

Businesses should take note of where the two trends of the speed of business and enhanced online user behavioral changes merge turbulently. Employees, customers, and partners are getting used to working online, connecting to each other, and sharing on a level far beyond what e-mail access and the static content on Web sites provide. People are using these tools to collaborate in more ways than one-on-one communications. They are voicing their opinions to a larger audience through more channels of communication, across organizational lines both within and beyond the company. They are trying to overcome organizational silos, facilitate idea sharing and innovation, and build stronger relationships with fellow employees. By supporting these drives with software, social computing is now reshaping the process of organizational decision making.

This kind of collaborative effort points to new ways of looking at how employees work across teams, departments, geographies, time zones, and skill sets. It can happen anywhere at any time: directly between members who knowingly engage each other, indirectly between those who contribute to a group, or even incidentally in a shared environment when people working for their own goals reveal some bit of knowledge that can help others. Such interactions can last a few minutes, a few hours, a few days, or a few weeks, or might even continue to exist indefinitely as long as a need exists. Collaboration can bring together skills and knowledge in more permutations than members might have imagined.

Such complex networks of people across the enterprise and beyond (for instant, short, or even long-duration projects) hint at a new way of defining a "team" effort and how to manage and lead such effort. These groups might involve participants independent of the organizational structure, or they might stand entirely beyond the organization. Yet they can produce useful work and information that can help a cause.

These do not follow the traditional behaviors of high- and low-performing teams, as Jon R. Katzenbach and Douglas K. Smith described in the business classic *The Wisdom of Teams*.[8] Instead, a

---

[8] J. Katzenbach and D. Smith, *The Wisdom of Teams* (New York: Harper Collins, 1993).

revised look at the basis for high-performing individuals and groups now includes those who demonstrate social intelligence[9] and find the best ways to incorporate the wisdom of crowds.[10] Instead of focusing on direct people management, social computing centers on driving results through influence and indirect leadership. Working in this mode requires an understanding of the context of the social environment and applying the right techniques.

Social computing methods raise new questions about how to conduct business in the Internet age: What business problems can social computing methods address? Do they offer new opportunities or approaches to providing value to customers? Do these changes require new business models or changes to existing ones? To answer these questions, we need to look at how organizations are applying these social computing methods.

Integrating into Business Processes and Activities

Verizon's social computing applies to customer-support processes. Amazon focuses on increasing sales. IBM's InnovationJam combines research goals and corporate social responsibility activities. Best Buy's project combines market intelligence, inventory management, and sales planning. Other social environments, such as for Disney and Chacha.com, are business services to customers.

Amazon's recommendation system and IBM's InnovationJams are substeps of the overall business process—in these cases, the innovation process and the retail-sales process. In other instances, social computing methods are parallel or ancillary supportive steps to existing business processes, such as Verizon still providing official customer service in addition to the community-driven approach. Disney and Chacha.com's social computing activities comprise entire areas of business and include many processes within.

Social computing methods can seemingly apply anywhere in a single business and across industries. The recurring pattern seems to

---

[9] Daniel Goleman, *Social Intelligence: The New Science of Human Relationships* (New York: Bantam Books, July 2007). http://tinyurl.com/3pssto.

[10] James Suroweicki, *The Wisdom of Crowds* (New York: Random House, 2004).

be the set of social computing methods and the decision-making processes they support.

First, we need to recognize that many approaches exist to social computing. Each approach seeks to get a group of people to focus on a certain task. However, the way people interact in the group, and the approach to driving results, can vary with the task. Understanding the right mix of shared experience, leadership model, and task helps set the right context for a social computing project. This context sheds light on the expectations for the social computing project to both your organization and the potential participants. Getting results out of a social environment also requires an understanding of the culture of the social group and a plan for enabling the members of the group to participate in and act on the goals. You will also need ways to describe how these social computing activities deliver and impact your own business processes.

Summary

Businesses, large and small, are finding ways to involve employees, customers, and partners in shared, online, collaborative activities that perform distinct business functions. Such *social* computing methods replace pure computer hardware–based methods for analyzing complex information and supporting decision-making processes. These methods guide a diverse group of participants to focus on tasks that take advantage of the experience, expertise, and subjective analysis skills that they bring to the group. They can apply to a wide range of business areas and industries by providing collective effort and wisdom to support the underlying decision-making steps in these processes.

Achieving results from social computing involves looking beyond simply gathering a group of people together online. With the high-powered support available, it can be relatively easy to bring people to the stage. The challenge lies in getting a widely diverse group to contribute to the actual performance of social computing. This takes a coherent effort to create a defined context for the social computing activity, generate an enablement plan to guide it, and establish a measurement approach to show how both the participants and the organization benefit.

2

Sharing a Social Experience

Music Web site *last.fm* offers the equivalent of radio stations on the Web, with a particular social aspect that provides innovative customer value: Whenever a listener chooses or plays a song, last.fm detects the choice of artist and song, and uses this as input to future recommendations. To re-create the continuous streaming experience of traditional radio stations, the site automatically chooses the next song to play to the listener by using the collective preferences and choices of its members to suggest similar artists and bands, to deliver a better customer experience.[1] This moves well beyond traditional music stations, with songs and artists chosen by a staff of DJs based on a combination of their personal, expertly guided choices; what music promoters actively set before them; and perhaps selections provided by their parent company network. C. K. Prahalad and M. S. Krishnan describe in *The New Age of Innovation*[2] how supporting this capability for users to customize their experience creates opportunities for the customer and you're the organization to share in innovation.

If last.fm used only the listener's own choices to make recommendations, it would lose the social involvement and instead be just a personal experience. The transformation to a social experience occurs when last.fm examines the patterns of similar choices across many users: The recommendation for a listener's next song is then based on what other users may have picked after the previous choice. The site adds value to the customer by applying social information to guide an

---

[1] The site is located at http://last.fm. Though unusual, this is a valid Web address—adding .com or other suffixes to it is not necessary.
[2] C. K. Prahalad and M. S. Krishnan, *The New Age of Innovation* (New York: McGraw-Hill, 2008).

individual's choices, making it easier for the customer to find similar music. This puts the site two steps ahead of traditional broadcast radio, with both customized choices for each individual and socially guided recommendations.

In the last.fm model, users make selections from a large set of products; those selections then influence their own or others' future decisions. Other online retail sites, such as Amazon.com, the Netflix movie-rental service, and retailer Target.com,[3] use this same model. These sites often take a structured approach to getting input from a social group, resulting in a *mass collaboration experience* aggregating many individual views into common streams of information.

As more customers make choices, those decisions contribute to the existing information about what selections people make, providing better information to each customer. In this way, such services can actually *increase* in usefulness and value as the number of participants increases. The value to the business rises as customers make more choices and, hopefully, more purchases.

The input that a person gets from other users of a Web site is the hallmark of a social environment. This input—or, rather, the output that goes to someone else—does not have to be direct; it can go through filters, transformations, or aggregations with other information before it reaches another person. In the case of tracking "similar choices," the social value depends on aggregating the information from many people, indirectly collaborating *en masse*. In contrast, it is also possible to be social without aggregating any information, but by independently sharing information with others.

Slideshare provides a distinct online service that lets users share their slide presentations with others, a common need both inside businesses and when presenting at public events and conferences.[4] A user can post a presentation and indicate whether others can

---

[3] On Amazon.com, every product page lists a set of other products that people either examined or purchased, to encourage the customer to consider other purchases. Netflix shows other popular movie choices based on individual user choices as well as those from their city or local region. Target.com shows related products that other customers examined.

[4] The site, located at http://slideshare.net, is open to anyone who wants to join and post presentations.

download the document or only view it online. Other users can read, rate, and comment on the material, or share it with others. An added convenience is the capability to show a presentation on other Web sites, further increasing its visibility.

Unlike the last.fm example, each content item (slide) on Slideshare can stand on its own; slides do not need to be aggregated to provide value to users. Users post as many presentations as they like, focusing on their own interests even while sharing with others. Users do not even need to form relationships with other Slideshare users to get value from sharing. Therefore, while sharing with others, users are directing their friends or peers to an experience focused on social experience but centered on a user's individual identity. This same model is common in millions of single-author blogs on the Internet.[5] Every blogger builds an *individual experience* focused on the author's persona or interests.

Some social environments extend the individual's experience to emphasize a person's network of relationships. In these environments, each person provides content to share with others, but the value comes from the relationship network provided as a service of the context of the Web site. For instance, LinkedIn enables people to maintain and manage their network of business contacts online.[6] Unlike a traditional list of contacts, which you might store in desktop e-mail software such as Microsoft's Outlook, in an online e-mail service such as Google's gmail, or on your cellphone, the LinkedIn system brings together every member's network, enabling people to find and create new contacts through others.

Users either indicate whether they are willing to share their contacts with others or evaluate individual requests to establish a contact. In particular, this approach takes advantage of pathways between people; it enables a requestor to reach a target contact by asking each

---

[5] Blogs can have a single individual owner or share control among a group of users as a group blog. However, these are two different types of experiences. The sidebar "The Trouble with Flexible Social Software," later in this chapter, describes the significance of multiple experiences from a single tool.

[6] The site is located at www.linkedin.com. Anyone can create a profile, such as mine, www.linkedin.com/in/rawnshah. The owner of the profile can determine whether to share the contact network with others.

person along the path to bring him closer to the target. This is useful to just about any job role but is of particular interest to marketers, business development managers, and salespeople, who meet and need to meet many people in a single year. No more paper business cards or even online contact information files to pass around—it's all stored on LinkedIn.

LinkedIn has millions of users, but each person knows only his particular network of contacts, not everyone's. In other words, each person's social experience is primarily with his own social network.[7] Users can communicate with individuals in their network or with the entire network. Because users can add information about their expertise, as well as a resumé, they can learn more about each other. Public social sites such as Plaxo[8] or Facebook[9] support similar ideas, but they also enable users to designate others as a family member, a friend, a work contact, or another relationship, to qualify how users prefer to talk to them.

The value of LinkedIn comes from meshing many relationship networks, enabling users to discover and form new relationships they might not have otherwise made. This *social network experience* differs from the individual experience, in that communications are socially output only to members of your network instead of being open to anyone. This is useful when you want to have a conversation only with people in your relationship network.

In contrast to the person-centric approach of a social network, people frequently work on common goals in groups. Such a workgroup might have a leader, but it typically does not center on a single individual. The traditional view of a team within a specific hierarchy of an organization under one manager fits here, but so does the

---

[7] LinkedIn also includes a way to interact with a group of people, through LinkedIn Groups, but for this discussion, let's focus on the basic social network experience of LinkedIn.

[8] Plaxo is available at www.plaxo.com.

[9] Is Facebook an individual experience or a social network? The Web site, at www.facebook.com, can support either position: Users can restrict access to their profile to only their social network, or can alternatively open it to anyone and everyone. Most people refer to Facebook as a social network, to emphasize the relationship building.

concept of workgroups with members from multiple teams with different managers.

IBM Lotus Quickr is a social software tool designed to allow workgroups to share documents, coordinate calendars, and assign and track tasks.[10] The software supports this classic model of team or workgroup collaboration, acting as a common container for all the products of members' joint or combined efforts. These products are stored in a common context instead of being stored individually on each member's computer, making it easier for group members to understand and keep track of the shared activities. In closed workgroups, a member must be invited to the social environment, and what that member shares is generally kept private to the group.

However, some workgroups might need to share their work with others, while still preserving their core group members as the "team" behind the information. They can do this by assigning some team members the core workgroup rights, to perform functions such as creating, editing, and deleting, while allowing others only to read or provide comments. This distinction creates two classes of people with identities of "the workgroup members" and "everyone else," which has its own benefits and consequences.

A visible workgroup of music experts at Pandora.com, another online radio station, performs the job of categorizing music (as in last.fm). Although both Pandora and last.fm are online radio stations with similar goals of providing guided choices personalized to each user's tastes, they go about it in different ways. Pandora is an outgrowth of the Music Genome Project,[11] an organized approach meant to categorize any type of recorded music according to distinguishing qualities. For example, a song might have a particular lyrical style, harmony, use of instruments, and genre. In all, several hundred factors describe a "genome" for any piece of music. Pandora examines each user's direct selections of artists or songs and tracks the

---

[10] IBM Lotus Quickr is part of the family of social computing tools IBM offers—see www-01.ibm.com/software/lotus/category/network/.

[11] Pandora Media's service is available at www.pandora.com. You can find out more about the Music Genome Project on Wikipedia at http://en.wikipedia.org/wiki/Music_Genome_Project.

commonalities in these genomic factors of their preferences. Users are also offered other selections and asked to rate them, to further determine their taste preferences.

The primary social aspect of Pandora comes from the collective work of the group of musical experts who work together to describe the qualities of each piece of music. The results from this core group's efforts factor into the decision-support system of Pandora music, provided to all its customers.[12]

Whether restricted to use by only its own members or openly visible to others, after a certain point, a core group can become too large for everyone to know or work closely with each other. The tightly knit experience of a small circle breaks down, but a different form of value can emerge from this larger entity of a community experience.

Software technology vendor SAP's Developer Network provides a community in which members can reach out to each other to get advice on issues they face or to gather information on new features or products.[13] The nature of complex enterprise applications, such as the one from SAP, means that it might be impossible for a vendor to describe all the possible problems a customer could run into. There are simply too many permutations of the vendor's own software, along with other systems and databases in the organization to integrate with. However, large vendors have many customers who come across similar situations, so these customers can help each other. As an example, SAP's Developer Network, open to anyone who wants to direct a question to other members, can potentially reduce support calls, as well as uncover new methods or practices directly from customers.

Some might consider the changing list of members and not knowing all other members in a community experience as a disadvantage. Although some subset of the members could stay the same over the

---

[12] Pandora also enables users to share their collections of music, pointing to a second social experience: an individual experience model, similar to sharing a collection of presentations on Slideshare.

[13] The SAP Developer Network (SDN), at https://www.sdn.sap.com/irj/sdn, is open to everyone and provides a number of social computing services. The example in this book centers on the discussion forums.

long-term, this open-ended possibility makes the community experience continually evolving, both an advantage and a challenge at the same time. Thus, participating in a community is different from interacting in a workgroup because it introduces greater unknowns about others—including their expertise, skills, experience, and opinions or positions on different matters—and usually relies on weaker relationships between members. However, a larger membership offers greater diversity of ideas and perspectives. Additionally, in many circumstances, a community approach is needed instead of a workgroup approach simply because of the number of people involved.

In contrast to the indirectness of mass collaborations, such as in the last.fm example, communities are necessary when the identity and background of people matter in decision making. Whom you get advice from in the SAP Developer Network can make a big difference when you need to rely on another member's recommendation. Therefore, understanding others' experiences and seeing some demonstration or getting references from others can strengthen a recommendation. Here, people need to interact more directly with each other than in a mass collaboration because identity and role make a difference. A person's identity and reputation, as well as his history of direct contact with the requestor, enhances the output of the social environment. Also, unlike workgroups and social networks, how someone communicates to a public community might be different from what that person would say to his direct contacts. Relationships can be weaker in general, so greater emphasis falls on finding commonality and shared interests. Hence, the topic or purpose of the community becomes the center of the experience, often with members pursuing many possible goals within the overall theme.

Modeling Social Experiences

The previous examples have distinguished some of the models for social experiences commonly found in different types of social software tools (see Table 2.1). Another type of experience also can transform into a social one (see the sidebar "Nonsocial Experiences").

TABLE 2.1   Social Experience Models

Social Experience Model	Example	Description
Individual	Slideshare, blogs	Each member has an environment where they can share their ideas and knowledge, visible to all other users in the same domain.
Social network	LinkedIn, Plaxo, Facebook	Each person has a select network of direct relationships with other users they can collaborate with. To work with others outside this network, the user first must form relationships with them.
Closed workgroup	Lotus Quickr	A select group of members collaborate on ideas and experiences among themselves within a dedicated space.
Visible workgroup	Pandora/ The Music Genome Project	A select group of members collaborate and contribute ideas and experiences within a dedicated space, but they also selectively allow other users to access their information.
Community	SAP Developer Network	Any member can join the group, to contribute to or read the information within the dedicated space. Many communities can exist within the overall domain, and users can join any of these.
Mass collaboration	"Similar choices" on last.fm, Amazon.com, or Target.com	Anyone can contribute to or read the information in the space. Membership is not necessary to contribute. Beyond individual information, the experience aggregates their inputs into collective results.

These *social experience models* are not just an aspect of their social environments—they're instrumental to how they deliver their value. These models serve a distinctive purpose in how they enable relationships or focus users to work on a task. They also describe different roles for participants in the social environment, indicating who can provide input, who controls the direction of the work, and who gains the benefit of the output.

All these models have several generic roles: the visitor, the member, the leader, the owner, and the sponsor. These roles come in handy when trying to distinguish the abilities or involvement of different people in a social environment.

Nonsocial Experiences

Aside from the social experiences listed in Table 2.1, another variety of digital experience can potentially become social. In the last.fm example, you saw that if the content customization were limited to each user without any kind of sharing involved, this would become a *personal* experience for each user, not a social one. This personal experience model is important to keep in mind because, although many Web sites today are possibly customizable for users, they are not social. Yet such personal experience sites are possible starting points for a social computing project. The last.fm example shows this transition implemented when the individual customer choices are shared as collective input along with the input of other users. High-fashion retailer Coach provides an expertly crafted online store[14] where anyone can browse collections or purchase items. However, this is, by design, an individual shopping experience, with no input from other shoppers on what items they prefer or why—this is an entirely personal experience, not a social one.

Visitors often come to social environments to investigate or participate without establishing their identities. Depending on what access and capabilities are granted to this role, the visitors might be able to just read basic information. When visitors establish their identities—for example, by creating an account in that environment—they become distinctly identifiable *members*. Not all social experience models require an identity to perform actions—in this case, members are essentially identical to visitors. However, sharing an identity communicates a longer-term interest in the environment and distinguishes a person as one with whom others can build a relationship.

All social experiences have leaders as direct or indirect influencers on the social group. The owner—or owners—of a social group has administrative control over the software behind the environment. This means that the social group owners can manage the content or membership, if needed. Because of this level of control, the owners

---

[14] You can access the Coach online store at www.coach.com.

can make leadership choices and decisions for all others involved in the social environment. (We return to the topic of leadership in Chapter 3, "Leadership in Social Environments.")

These benefits arise from the activities in the environment, but the various roles have to work for it. Successful social environments focus on delivering the appropriate value to all roles in a balanced manner (see Table 2.2). Providing value to members without returning some value to leaders or sponsors eventually results in a lack of leadership or support for the environment. On the other hand, focusing on delivering just to sponsors without benefiting members eventually results in poor participation and poor results. Similarly, when all the focus is on building up the prominence of the leaders but not delivering to members, the environment simply becomes a vanity piece. As with the actions of circus performers spinning many plates on sticks, the balance of a social environment is not about trying to spin one plate faster than the other ones, but about paying equal attention to each of them.

TABLE 2.2   Sources of Value in Experiences to Owners, Members, and Sponsors

	How the Owners or Leaders Benefit	**How Visitors or Members Benefit**	**How the Sponsors or Organization Benefit**
Personal	Through the value of the content offered to them	Not applicable	Through top-down distribution of content to users
Personal social network	By building contacts and relationships with others	Depends on how they value the expertise or relationship of the owner	By enabling relationship building across members, to further individual development and knowledge sharing
Individual	By demonstrating their personal expertise, interests, and actions to draw a network of relationships with others	Initially through value from the owner's content, followed by the longer-term relationship value	By providing individuals the opportunity to build their skills or expertise and helping to identify prospective leaders that connect well with others

TABLE 2.2 Sources of Value in Experiences to Owners, Members, and Sponsors

	How the Owners or Leaders Benefit	How Visitors or Members Benefit	How the Sponsors or Organization Benefit
Closed group	By developing an invited group to focus efforts on an activity or topic, and by building stronger relationships with members	Through shared group efforts and relationships within the group	By focusing on the competence and experience of group members on a specific activity, and enabling deeper relationships directly between the members
Visible group	By developing an invited group to focus efforts on an activity or topic, by building stronger relationships with group members, and by demonstrating their efforts to a wider population	Through shared efforts and relationships within the group, and exposure of their combined efforts to a wider population	By focusing on the competence and experience of group members on a specific activity, building deeper relationships directly between members, and building extended relationships with others
Community	By bringing in diverse perspectives and new opportunities and relationships	Through the value of the collectively gathered or analyzed content, and the help of other members	By creating an open invitation to allow members to self-organize and deliberate around a focused topic or interest
Mass collaboration	Same as for sponsors	Through the value of the collectively gathered or analyzed content	By focusing a population to build consensus around specific activities

Different Experiences for a Complex World

Social environments can be much more complex than shown in the examples at the beginning of this chapter. Many social environments implement multiple experience models, combined into different parts of the environment. This enables the environments to capitalize on different tasks when individual users require a particular type of experience. For example, Amazon.com's online store provides individual experiences in which users can create "plogs" (product blogs), where authors can write about their products and what they are working on. As a company, Amazon.com also provides a set of

The Trouble with Flexible Social Software

The flexible nature of some social software tools can also work against the intended use or goal of a social environment. Social software can confuse members when the software supports multiple social experience models that differ only in configuration. For example, a wiki (a collection of Web pages designed to enable anyone with access to contribute or modify content) is a particularly versatile type of social software tool that enables one or more users to collaboratively edit a document on the Web. These can be particularly confusing because the same wiki software can be configured in several ways, each using a different experience model:

- I use the wiki as an online word processor to create and save documents that only I can read—an entirely personal nonsocial experience.

- I use this wiki as a tool to create and manage content only for myself, but I might allow specific others in my personal network of relationships to read it—a social network experience.

- Only I can edit the information, but I openly share it with everyone in my company so they can give feedback on my ideas—an individual experience.

- I invite and limit participation to a core permanent group of members to contribute to or read the information—a closed workgroup experience.

- I invite a core permanent team of contributors, but I allow anyone to read the information—a visible group experience.

- I open the wiki for anyone to read or contribute to at any time—a community or mass collaboration experience.

The concept of a wiki is so dynamic that it is overloaded with possibilities. On entering a wiki environment that doesn't identify its particular model and intent, users can easily misunderstand the model and its intended use, causing frustration and, in turn, discouraging participation.

business services entirely separate from its retail store: Amazon Web Services. Here, other tools implement social experiences, which we examine in Chapters 4, "Social Tasks: Collaborating on Ideas," and 5, "Social Tasks: Creating and Managing Information."

Other social software makes creating and maintaining social environments additionally complex because the environments become capable of supporting different experiences, each depending on the configuration. For example, within IBM, thousands of wikis exist for various individuals, groups, teams, or projects; each wiki implements an individual, closed workgroup, visible workgroup, community, or even mass collaboration experience, depending on the needs of the owners. However, as you can see from the sidebar "The Trouble with Flexible Social Software," trouble can arise from selecting a social software application without defining the goals of the environment.

Summary

Social collaboration occurs within various contexts in a shared social experience. Each type of experience provides its own value to the owner of a social environment, its members, or its sponsors; you can apply each experience in a different manner. A handful of archetypes exist as common models of these social experiences: social network, individual usage, closed workgroup, visible workgroup, community, or mass collaboration. In addition, the nonsocial personal experience model, a precursor to these others, is common to many Web sites.

By applying these social experience models, we can better understand the purpose of the roles and relationships between people in the environment, their activities and culture of working together, and the necessary leadership within these environments. Selecting a social experience model also depends on other factors of the social computing task that is placed before the participants, and one factor is the particular model for leadership that can guide members to work on tasks. We take a look at leadership models next.

3

Leadership in Social Environments

Jimmy Wales is famous for founding Wikipedia, the largest free encyclopedia on the Web. But fewer people recall his project before that, Nupedia, which had a similar goal of providing encyclopedia content for free on the Internet. Wikipedia's success is evident in its millions of users and entries, and in supporting 55 languages as varied as Vietnamese, Arabic, and Russian, all submitted by volunteers across the Internet. Its success might even have helped shutter Microsoft's MSN Encarta, a leading commercial competitor.[1] By the time Wales's Nupedia effort closed down after about three years of operation, the site had 24 published articles, with 74 others in review.[2] By comparison, Wikipedia reached about 200,000 articles in the same amount of time.[3]

Why did two efforts to produce online encyclopedias involving some of the same leaders end so differently? The difference lies mostly in how these systems reviewed and published articles, and in who made those decisions. The Nupedia model followed the traditional peer-review process for publishing academic articles, faithfully followed by encyclopedia publishers for more than a century—but this time in an online venue. Wikipedia tried a different approach: Let anyone contribute an article—give enough people opportunity to

---

[1] MSN Encarta, "Important Notice: MSN Encarta to Be Discontinued," http://encarta.msn.com/guide_page_FAQ/FAQ.html.

[2] Wikipedia, "Nupedia," as accessed on 1 May 2009, http://en.wikipedia.org/wiki/Nupedia.

[3] Wikipedia, "Wikipedia: Statistics," as accessed on 1 May 2009, http://en.wikipedia.org/wiki/Wikipedia:Statistics.

participate in its development, and the "best" article would emerge. Content quality control became a dynamic process based on how interested parties would edit or make changes to the material, without limitations on review time, degree of change, or other factors. This defining change in how people could make decisions on the content and direction of the site—a *leadership model* that allowed anyone to become an editor and leader—drove Wikipedia's overwhelming success.

Not everyone publishes on Wikipedia, of course. Many people prefer an independent platform for their ideas. The millions of blogs on the Internet are a testament that individuals still want to voice their own opinions independently and perhaps lead their own conversations. Unlike Wikipedia, where numerous authors consolidate their thoughts into one set of results, individual blogs allow each person to speak independently. Wikipedia itself is one gigantic social environment with common rules for all. The success of each blog is a result of the leadership of its owners, who independently set the rules for what to publish and who can contribute. As such, individual blogs and Wikipedia have distinctively different leadership models.

How do these two social environment types compare to leadership in corporations and other organizations? For starters, blogs and Wikipedia emphasize the role of individuals—their ambitions, preferences, competitive spirit, interactive behavior, personal characteristics, interests, and personal goals. In contrast, most organizations still try to manage themselves through centralized, hierarchical structures, forged in the days of ancient empires. This command-oriented structure emphasizes predictable and standardized processes to manage an operational environment, while deemphasizing individual expression and direction.

Social environments can be managed either in the style of the sponsoring organization or as an independent entity with an autonomous leadership. Wikipedia's example represents how its sponsoring foundation manages itself. In contrast, employees in many companies author blogs from their company Web site or on their own, but this does not necessarily mean that they are mouthpieces for their employer. How they lead their blogs is independent from the management style of their employers.

This does not eliminate the possibility of centralized leadership in social environments. Rather, it suggests the need to separate the authority of organizational sponsors from authority in the social environment. It allows the owners of each social environment to choose how transparent they want to be in their decisions and operations (see the sidebar "Transparency in Social Environments and Organizations").

Transparency in Social Environments and Organizations

Is transparency a strategic advantage? Consider the fact that most social environments compete for the attention of existing and potential members. An environment with greater transparency enables people to determine at an earlier stage whether the social group meets their interest. As a strategy to draw more members, transparency offers advantages over other groups that restrict information.

Selecting a particular leadership model does not necessarily exclude the possibility of *transparency*, or clear insight into the workings, issues, and possibly even strategies of a social environment. Transparency adds a dimension that enables members to evaluate and analyze the workings and leadership of a social environment, in terms of the goals and the cultural values of the group (see Chapter 7, "Building a Social Culture"). The greater the transparency, the easier it is for members to decide whether decisions and directions meet their expectations and agree with their shared cultural values. Often, however, cultural values are open to interpretation, and even when the leaders consider that their actions are in line with the values of the group, other members might not agree. In a transparent situation, that can lead to disagreements and disharmony.

Creating a transparent social environment that is autonomous (free standing) from the sponsoring business is one strategy for creating a limited venue that can share more openly, especially for businesses that need to be fairly opaque.

Governance and Leadership Models

No single form of governance or leadership can reach across something as large as the Internet. Each social environment is its own microcosm, with its own population, activities, goals, and direction, within larger networks such as the Internet or a corporate intranet. Social environments can thus range from being strongly centralized to being entirely decentralized leadership control models.

Leadership models and governance in social environments are not always formally introduced or established. They often emerge naturally, as a result of people working together in a social group. Over time, as populations grow, members might seek new patterns to coordinate some of their efforts. As they tackle these efforts, they lay the basis for leadership, acceptable behavior, and direction for the social group. This implies some form of governance, however formal or informal, in guiding that population.

Whether planned from the beginning or as an eventual outcome of organizing a social group, each model of leadership offers particular advantages or sets limitations or predispositions to governance mechanisms. Therefore, it's important to understand these leadership models by themselves.

Leadership models encompass several ideas:

- **How do you select leaders?** This model emphasizes who can lead a particular social group and focuses on the nature and expression of their authority. Additionally, it relates to how those leaders are selected and who can be part of the selection process.

- **How can people participate?** Who decides who can participate and the format of their participation? Does everyone participate on the same equal level, or do different strata of distinctions exist?

- **How do you set goals and direction?** Who can define the goals, tasks, and direction of the group? Who can change them? How do nonleaders have an impact on the direction for the social group?

These ideas focus on the question of authority—who leads a social group. Although the steps to establish authority vary, they tend to be based on a few archetypal leadership models. These leadership models then rely on *governance processes and policies,* a subject in Chapter 9, "Community and Social Experience Management." These processes and policies consider the myriad issues in the day-to-day running of the social group and environment, covering technical aspects (such as managing membership and access controls, editing or deleting information, and so on) and human issues (such as defining acceptable behavior, arbitrating debates and contentions, encouraging participation, training and educating members, and communicating cultural values).

After selecting a leadership model, identifying the processes and policies to fit into that model becomes easier. Both the leadership model and the processes and policies have an impact on how members participate. But processes and policies are relatively easier to change than the leadership model. In the physical world, this is analogous to changing laws in a country versus shifting from a democracy to a monarchy.

A Selection of Leadership Models

The leadership models in Table 3.1 describe the variety of archetypes on enterprise networks and across the Internet. They are independent of social software tools and products themselves, which opens the choices available. Each model allows a business to choose, based on its own readiness level, whether to adopt social software to share control, leadership, participation, and direction.

We look at several government models in the following sections, including the *centralized* (and the slightly different *centralized-with-input*) model, *delegated, representative, starfish,* and *swarm* models. After we examine the following leadership models, we look at how they fit together with social experience models.

The Centralized Models

The centralized model is the closest to traditional top-down business management. In this model, the owners of the environment

TABLE 3.1   Social Government Models

Type	Leader Selection	Participation	Direction	Social Environment Example
Centralized	Leaders are selected by sponsors and can transfer leadership to anyone they choose.	Leaders have total control over all content in the environment—this is not quite a social environment.	Leaders have total control over direction.	A traditional Web site, with perhaps a personal tone
Centralized with input	Leaders are selected by sponsors and can transfer leadership to anyone they choose.	Leaders have majority or total control over the content, but they enable users to add secondary input, such as feedback and comments.	Leaders have total control over direction.	A standard individual or group blog, or a wiki editable by only a core team
Delegated	Leaders are selected by sponsors and can transfer leadership to anyone they choose.	Leaders share control and enable others to enter input, but still have the option to control or edit this input.	Leaders have majority control over direction.	A single community on Ning.com, vendor-supported forums or wikis, or many corporate workgroups
Representative	The membership elects leaders. Leaders can nominate others but cannot assign leadership without election.	All members have equal capabilities and rights to participate, but leaders might have additional administrative control over the environment.	Leaders have equally shared control over direction.	Large industry standards workgroups, such as the Internet Engineering Task Force and the World Wide Web Consortium

TABLE 3.1 Social Government Models

Type	Leader Selection	Participation	Direction	Social Environment Example
Starfish	Leadership is purely voluntary from members.	Everyone has equal basis and capabilities, but members agree to follow some general principles, rules, or ideologies.	Leaders have no control, or little but localized pockets of control.	Wikipedia, which enables anyone to input or edit, but has a structure for how the contents are organized; activity-based computing
Swarm	No explicit leadership exists. Leadership is purely based on influence.	Everyone has equal basis to provide input, with either only a basic definition of the input format or no definition.	No single individual has overwhelming control over direction; the direction is aggregated through the combined effect of the swarm.	Digg.com enables anyone to vote on items, creating a sorted list of news for the social group

aim to put together information and share it with an audience, but they prefer to retain control of contributions, goals, and directions taken within their particular environment. The owners might enable the audience to send feedback directly to the environment, but the owners choose whether to share this feedback openly. This is common to most traditional Web sites that focus on delivering organizationally produced content directly to an audience, such as news or magazine publishers, online retail sites, and corporate informational sites.

A variation of this centralized model occurs when social interaction starts to enter the picture. The owners still create primary information that makes up the majority of the content in the social environment. However, the subtle but important distinction is that other users can also contribute their thoughts and views as visible secondary input, in the form of comments, notes, annotations, or other feedback. This opens the opportunity for some basic level of interaction by a social group, even when the owners still maintain control.

The same examples of traditional Web sites (publishers, retail sites, corporate sites) have started to incorporate this degree of open feedback. For example, CNN.com and Businessweek.com's main site allows feedback as comments and polls, but users cannot write an original article without their consent. LinkedIn, described in Chapter 2, "Sharing a Social Experience," allows members to directly manage their own business profiles and contact networks. Although each network has many individuals as members, the owners can decide whom they want to allow into their network.

The benefit of this modification to the centralized model is that it provides a way for a group of people, beyond the core, to collaborate and exchange ideas among themselves. It also differentiates the contributions of the owners from those of other community members. The only drawback of the model is that it doesn't set everyone at an equal or peer status. Essentially, it is still a place for the owners to lead with their ideas.

Many organizations still find the *centralized-with-input* model a "safe" starting point for an initial foray into social computing. The leaders of the social environment are usually representatives that the organization trusts. However, the invitation to provide secondary input welcomes the community to share thoughts.

Before you think of this as an unpopular approach, consider that most individual blogs tend to follow the centralized-with-input model. The blogger holds most of the conversation, while others can only comment. Those who post comments might influence the decisions of the owners or other readers, but they still have to defer to the wishes of the blogger.

The Delegated Model

The delegated model moves toward greater social interaction by enabling non-owners to provide their own primary input, assist in execution, or guide the direction. The owners are still involved, but cooperation and coordination occur with some others, often hierarchically below the owners. These delegates might come from a different organization than that of the owners who sponsor the social environment.

For succession of leadership among the delegates, the owners choose a replacement, possibly from recommendations by other delegates. For example, if the delegates are representatives of several teams, a replacement for an outgoing delegate might come from another member of the same team. Alternatively, the owners might choose new delegates on their own.

A typical example of a delegated model is a group blog that names each participating owner with every post. For example, BoingBoing.Net[4] provides news and commentary on Internet culture and names several key delegates as coeditors: Mark Fraunfelder, Cory Doctorow, David Pescovitz, Xeni Jardin, and John Battelle. Chris Anderson's book *The Long Tail*[5] describes how this group blog competes for readership with the likes of news powerhouses such as *The Wall Street Journal*. From time to time, the BoingBoing bloggers also invite guests to participate and publish entries. Not all group blogs follow the delegated leadership model. *PostSecret,*[6] a social commentary group blog, allows anyone to post anonymously to the blog, making it more a swarm leadership model.

Forum discussion communities sponsored by companies might also exhibit this model. In such communities, the sponsor assigns one or more employees to lead the environment. Those employees then invite specific participating members to become delegates for the rest. For example, the science periodical *Scientific American* offers "Ask the Experts," in which any user can submit any science question. Any number of other users vote on priorities for the submitted questions, and the editorial team routes the questions to appropriate experts or existing articles that respond to the queries.[7] Essentially,

---

[4] You can read the fairly frequent blog entries from BoingBoing at www.boingboing.net.

[5] Chris Anderson, *The Long Tail: Why the Future of Business is Selling Less of More* (New York: Hyperion 2006)

[6] The PostSecret social media project is published at www.postsecret.com.

[7] The "Ask the Experts" feature is available on *Scientific American* magazine's Web site at www.sciam.com/askexpert_directory.cfm.

this delegates the responsibility of covering a host of scientific topics across many designated experts.

The Representative Model

The representative model enables the membership to elect a core set of leaders to represent their interests for the overall direction of the social group. The election process might be well defined or loose, but its existence differentiates this model from the delegated or centralized model. This is typically a democratic election, open to any members and voted on by some or all of the members. The decisions for the social environment become the responsibility of these elected leaders.

In this model, most members have equal capability to participate and post in the environment. However, they have delegated leadership responsibilities, such as establishing the topic focus or providing direction to the representatives. Members don't always have to agree with the leadership's choices and direction: Those who object strongly (and fail to be part of the leadership) either can become hidden influencers or splinter off into their own group elsewhere if they can gain enough supporters. Leaders cannot pass on their mantle of leadership to others they choose directly; the general membership still must elect future leaders.

The 125-year-old professional technical organization IEEE (originally an acronym for the Institute for Electrical and Electronic Engineers, it now covers many other technology disciplines as well) supports its 375,000 members worldwide through many chapters and branches both in physical locations and online.[8] The discussion forums and online communities that it supports reflect the representative governance and leadership model of the overall organization. That is, leaders of forums come from the leaders of various chapters and subgroups. Any member can volunteer and eventually work up to becoming a leader.

---

[8] IEEE, "About the IEEE," published at www.ieee.org/web/aboutus/home/index.html.

The Starfish Model

The name of this model comes from the ideas of decentralized structures defined in the book *The Starfish and the Spider*.[9] The starfish model—and, later, the swarm model—is based on leaderless organizations in which no central group defines the structure of the overall social system. The starfish and swarm models come "closer" to the idea of democracy in its purest form, with every member getting an equal voice in every matter. This idea isn't just for small groups; it can have a fairly substantial population, with many subset groups, subchapters, or regional or topical affiliations. In the offline world, this sometimes leads to cumbersome deliberation by many members, but it is not impossible. *The Starfish and the Spider* gives the example of Alcoholics Anonymous—a starfishlike organization across North America and other countries that is leaderless but has more than 2 million members.

The key idea of the starfish model is that, although it is decentralized, the members willingly follow an organizing set of principles, ideas, or processes. This usually applies to a group context instead of an individual context. All members often are equal; any roles in the group simply exist to facilitate interaction instead of to give strict leadership direction over the group.

Open source application-development projects, such as Apache or Mozilla, started in principle with starfish approaches. The Apache Foundation started initially to cover its namesake Apache Web server, the most popular vendor-independent Web server software application available on the Internet. The Foundation has expanded to support many other projects, each of which typically comes under the starfish model.

Although starfish-governed environments are decentralized, they still depend on direct interaction among members to create consensus. The next model takes to an extreme the concept of aggregating the views of many members.

---

[9] O. Brafman and R. A. Beckstrom, *The Starfish and the Spider* (New York: Portfolio Press, 2006).

The Swarm Model

The swarm model might have only the slightest of common principles, ideas, or processes that bring people together. Aside from the high-level purpose, any member can perform some common structured actions, such as voting, rating, or submitting information. This model comes closest to a pure democracy and can suffer or benefit—depending on your viewpoint—from a constantly shifting focus. Because of their instantaneous and cross-population democratic approach, swarms excel at identifying trend behavior in a social group.

In nature, swarms exist by instinctual actions: A colony of ants can hunt for food in a seemingly anarchic fashion, yet still have some method to their madness. For example, when the ant colony needs more food, a random number of ants might take it upon themselves to go foraging beyond the anthill for food. As they go off, each in their own directions, they leave chemical pheromone signals indicating the way they went. Some ants might follow, while others go off in other directions. When an ant returns with food, it leaves a different message on the trail. Other ants see the signal and start to follow; eventually, they set off an overall signal that the food is "this way." Initially, the trail toward the food might be winding, but as successive ants find shorter routes, their combined messages create a stronger "this way" message for others to follow. Eventually, the others adapt to follow the shortest trail.[10]

The argument that people are not like ants is immaterial. With each person taking individual action, the collective is seemingly "organized" along actions that a majority of them hold in consensus, thereby setting the overall activity and direction of the social system. It can converge toward a single major activity, diverge in different directions, or wind around.

---

[10] Eric Bonabeau and Guy Theraulaz, "Swarm Smarts," *Scientific American* online (March 2000). Accessible at www.sciamdigital.com/index.cfm?fa=Products.ViewIssuePreview&ARTICLEID_CHAR=AB97C110-6A49-42A2-90F8-ED14E26FFDB. This is not universal behavior in all ants. Some also use other methods to find their way—for example, Nigel Franks and Tom Richardson, "Teaching in Tandem-Running Ants," Nature vol 439 (12 January 2006): pg 153–153. Accessible at http://www.nature.com/nature/journal/v439/n7073/full/439153a.html.

As a strategy, it simply *works* without any overall coordination or bureaucratic decision-making or guiding processes. There is simply no need for such processes. This might seem chaotic and is often hard to grasp, but within that chaos are areas of self-organization. The appeal of this leadership model comes from its simplicity and lack of strong oversight. However, some common actions are needed for the activity to be cohesive.

Some types of social software emphasize the swarm model. For example, a social tagging (folksonomy) method enables users to individually associate a Web location with a term of their own choice, but the overall system aggregates common terms across users and combines the overall set of Web locations. Therefore, the swarm behavior of individual users driven by their own reasons contributes to productive overall decisions.

In terms of social management, the swarm model can depend greatly on influence—either of the participants or of the strength or importance of the ideas themselves. For example, the online news site Digg.com enables each person to vote on a particular news item, filtering across a collective basis the important news of the moment. However, as prominent "diggers" know, some members can influence others to vote on their item, thereby raising its prominence.

The benefits of this model are flexibility and adaptability—it generally follows the pulse of participating members. Given an objective set of choices, it is possible to determine what people consider the most significant. The downside is that, to minimize the impact of a few top influencers, a site needs a large population of participants. This model also more easily follows objective ideas than subjective ones. The more subjective the actions or ideas are for members to consider, the less likely it is that the swarm will converge toward an overall result.

Choosing a Leadership Model

Choosing a leadership model can lead to four different states: a formally defined model; an informal, loosely described model; a *de facto* state; or an indeterminate state. You might assume that choosing no model would automatically result in the *de facto* state, as commonly used in the rest of the industry. However, this can be confusing when multiple possibilities exist.

For example, individuals who create a blog to share their thoughts and communicate their ideas generally assume that they, or people they pick, are the only ones who can post ideas, thereby defaulting to themselves as the central authority of the blog. However, some social tools allow for multiple possibilities, and making no choice puts the leadership model in an indeterminate state.

For example, as Chapter 2 describes, wikis are generally a way to share the responsibilities of editing a document with a group—yet they allow for a variety of social experiences and leadership models. The leaders might choose to limit the ability to edit or change the content while allowing others to read; in contrast, users may assume that they have a right to edit as well. Users who enter a wiki come with their own expectations of how the wiki will operate, particularly who is allowed to participate.

Leadership models define the authority of leaders in a social environment, but we need to combine this with other concepts to create a more accurate picture, especially with the concept of social experience models. Most experience models have multiple choices of possible leadership models (see Figure 3.1).

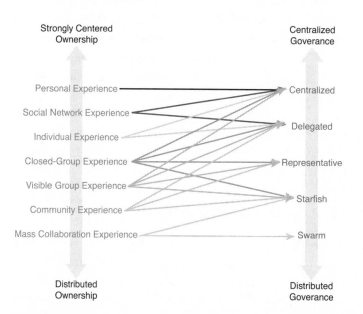

Figure 3.1   Mapping social experience to social governance models

Social sites need not implement the pure versions of these pairs of models, but understanding the connection helps leaders define goals and governance processes. Some social systems fall somewhere in between two or more models. Wikipedia generally reflects the starfish model, in which anyone can edit and contribute. But a core of volunteers helps manage the "thought wars" that might break out for controversial topics; in such cases, the volunteer editors might lock down a page so that others cannot edit it. Some people view this as an aspect of the representative or delegate leadership model.

Some complex social environments offer the same population of members access to multiple social tools, each of which follows a different leadership model. For example, a single community site might have a discussion forum where anyone can start and lead discussions, while also hosting a blog where only designees of the community can do so.

Organizations that support an ecosystem or collection of many social environments could allow each to choose their own leadership models. In doing so, users should be aware of the possibility of variability and should keep in mind the model employed in each social environment.

Choosing a leadership model can also depend on the particular task you want the members to focus upon. Chapters 4, "Social Tasks: Collaborating on Ideas," and 5, "Social Tasks: Creating and Managing Information," take a closer look at the structure of these tasks for social environments and identify particular leadership models that work well for each. Consider the example of newsgathering through the help of a social group (also covered in more detail in Chapter 5). The Web site Slashdot.org provides daily updates of "news for nerds"—their description.[11] The editors of the site choose the news items from a wide range of submissions from their members, and they enable readers to comment on and discuss the news. Because of the editorial direction, it is similar to the hierarchical structure of traditional newspaper organizations, even though the "reporters" in this

---

[11] Slashdot.org describes itself as "News for Nerds" as part of its tag line. Accessible at http://slashdot.org. The name of the site is an anachronism from the structure of how files are stored in UNIX-like computer operating systems to indicate the topmost location.

case come from the audience of masses that contribute. By comparison, Digg.com focuses on similar topics but enables all members to vote on the best news instead of having a dedicated editorial team. The goals of the two sites are similar, yet they have radically different leadership models.

Both models have advocates. The idea that a set of knowledgable editors does some of the filtering for the audience helps build some confidence that it isn't filled with complete rubbish or, worse, spam. However, others see the Digg model as a better representation of what is important to many people instead of just a few key individuals. Both models take different approaches about who leads the overall focus of the conversations and, thus, steers the direction and social government of the site. Any business advantage of one model over the other is not yet clear; both are successes in their own right. However, achieving success in either model requires the leaders to understand the benefits of each model and consider appropriate techniques.

Leadership models might also evolve into another type. For example, it is easier for a particular social system to start as a delegate model and evolve toward a less strongly centered or more distributed leadership such as the representative or starfish model, when greater trust exists among the membership—enough that strong one-sided leadership is no longer required. However, the inverse—moving from a distributed starfish model toward a centralized one—typically does not occur. Such a change might be seen as an oppressive or controlling leadership move and might have drastic consequences on the members' participation or commitment level.

Governance in many social environments is often a fluid concept. Leadership models tend to solidify over time, but initially, the leaders and members can experiment with different approaches on how they want to work together. People generally see this as a good thing because it allows their voices to help shape the direction.

Leaders and Influencers

All long-running social groups with distinct identities have influencers in official or unofficial capacities. They help shape the direction of the social group and attainment of goals. Official leadership depends on how formal the group becomes in terms of defining governance of the group. Influence, on the other hand, can have little to do with what title you hold in your organization, where you work, or to whom you report.

As indicated earlier, as an autonomous group from the sponsoring organization, the structure of leadership can be radically different and even independent of the structure of the sponsoring organization. Chapter 7, "Building a Social Culture," takes a closer look at how the values of a parent or sponsoring organization can bleed into the social environment, especially when more of the members come from the same organization. Similarly, the leadership structure of the sponsoring organization can bleed into the social environment: Members might recognize their seniors from the organization and automatically defer to their leadership. The more heterogeneous the membership is across multiple organizations, the less this becomes a factor.

This raises the question of where influencers actually come from and whether influence is a *sticky* characteristic—after a person demonstrates influence in one social group, will that person continue to exhibit that behavior at all times or in other groups? Two leading minds take somewhat opposite stances on this topic. Malcolm Gladwell, author of *The Tipping Point*, describes key influential roles as inherent characteristics of certain people; they are naturally drawn to that kind of behavior, so they influence those around them with ideas they consider significant.[12] Duncan Watts, coauthor of *Six Degrees: The Science of a Connected Age*,[13] contends in his more recent research work[14] that influence does exist but is less a function of a few people in key roles and depends more on people who become influencers by accident when the right environmental situation arises for an idea to spread. However, both authors agree that people can

---

[12] See Chapter 2, "The Law of the Few," in Malcolm Gladwell's *The Tipping Point* (New York: Little, Brown & Co., 2000).

[13] Duncan J. Watts, *Six Degrees: The Science of a Connected Age* (New York: W. W. Norton & Co., 2004).

[14] Clive Thompson, "Is the Tipping Point Toast?" *Fast Company* online (February 2008). Thompson's article talks about Duncan Watts's new experiments in understanding how ideas spread in social groups.

become influential in specific matters and that detecting these influencers can help identify how the idea will spread and what shape it will take.

A number of ways can help identify influentials:

- Relationship networks can describe leadership, especially when they indicate a direction of interest. For example, members who have tens of thousands of followers on Twitter are inherently influential to some degree because they can easily communicate to a great many. Mapping these relationship networks can help identify other influencers simply in terms of how well connected or how frequently people turn to them for help.

- Some members might also intentionally take on prominent, unofficial, or self-declared roles as subject-matter experts or relationship brokers. Although not official leaders, they are well known or well connected, so they become influencers.

- Social environments that implement a way for members to collectively assign reputation to each other inherently identify influencers, as described by their high rankings or notable achievements.

- Social environments that implement a way for members to assign expertise areas can also identify influencers with different competencies.

With social software, it might seem easier to discover influence by tracking interactions. Unfortunately, accurately measuring the degree of influence and understanding this on a large scale remains an elusive goal. Even without understanding the true extent of leadership here, we can still examine where they are applied in different leadership models.

Summary

Leadership models, in conjunction with social experience models, help focus the purpose of the social environment. Leadership models offer different approaches to describing authority in a social environment, which helps shape the governance processes and policies. A variety of these models, such as the centralized, delegate, representative, starfish, and swarm models, are frequently used on the

Internet and within enterprises. These models vary based on how authority is concentrated within or distributed across the membership, by the mechanism for choosing leaders to set goals and direction, and by how members can participate in the social group. Not everyone directly states their choice of leadership models, but every social environment has one, even those that seem to have no identifiable leaders. Leaders can also choose to modify or evolve their model over time and in reaction to members' ideas and views. This fluid nature is typical in the early stages of a social environment's growth but tends to formalize over time.

4

Social Tasks: Collaborating on Ideas

Mars Incorporated—also known as Masterfoods outside North America—offers a way for people to personalize Mars products through its Web site, such as enabling users to add their own messages or images printed on the face of its famous M&Ms candy. I used the Mars offer to create personalized candy for our son's second birthday. However, the custom version I created with my son's photo and name is probably not something that I would want others to use. In this situation, although users can create their own custom versions, this isn't a task for users working or sharing collectively. In essence, this task is a personal experience, no matter how many people might repeat it each day.

In comparison, BurdaStyle, a site for sewing and clothing-design enthusiasts, enables members to not only create their own versions, but also share these ideas with others, to create outfits of their own. Users' capability to share their ingenuity and output with others illustrates the social aspect of this task.

Social groups radiate energy as a group, but harnessing and focusing this social power on a desired task requires some planning. As the differences between the approach of Mars and BurdaStyle suggest, a task for a social group is more than simply enabling a mass of people to engage in a task. It doesn't become social until the members of the group are *somehow* collectively interactive or involved in the overall process. How well you harness this social energy depends on the organization of the group and how you frame the task to perform.

Many social sites define these *social tasks* as part of a mission statement, activity, or goal for the group members. The social lending Web site Prosper implies in its name the goal for its members: to help each other prosper financially through social lending and borrowing. The Squidoo social site boldly declares, "Everyone's an expert at something"[1] and acts as a platform for people to share their expertise with knowledge seekers (the social task). Some social tools separate the task for members from the business objectives of the environment. For example, the children who play games and participate in Disney's Club Penguin do it for the entertainment, but Disney aims to deliver an entertainment platform as a commercial venture.

The Web site Web2list.com[2] identifies hundreds of social sites on the Internet, each with different approaches, technical implementations, and target populations, yet many sites have frequently repeating tasks and similar patterns. This chapter and the next aim to distinguish the different patterns of performing work in online social environments. These social task models might address only a subset of the possibilities across these hundreds of social sites, but they offer ways to understand the differences between models and the principles behind each model.

The Structure of Social Tasks

In contrast to the interpersonal, content, and environment actions that users can perform discretely, a social task is a larger view of collaborative work. Not all members might participate in the task, the tasks might not be assigned to specific members, the task might not need singular results, multiple tasks can exist in the same environment, and a variety of beneficiaries are possible. However, the task tries to get some possible permutation of the overall membership involved by asking members to provide input, perform some steps of a more complex task, make a decision, or consider or consume some information.

The dimensions of a social tasks model combine many of the ideas presented so far in this book, with a few additional concepts. Additionally, there are certainly other possible types of social tasks, derivatives, or variants that are not detailed in this book. This chapter

---

[1] On the front page of www.squidoo.com in August 2008.

[2] http://Web2list.com is a list generated by user contributions of hundreds of links to social and Web 2.0 sites.

provides a framework on how to define a social task and relate it to the other concepts from this book. The examples of tasks in this and the next chapter are here to guide you to develop your own methods using this framework.

Identifying Beneficiaries

The first identifying question is about the intended beneficiaries of the social task. Table 2.2 in Chapter 2, "Sharing a Social Experience" pointed out that members, owners, and sponsors can all simultaneously benefit from participating in a social environment. A social environment can have multiple tasks for its members, each of which can have a different beneficiary. Tasks can focus on short-term activities and benefits for members, compared to the long-term value of socially interacting in the environment. Members might be more willing to perform this work if they understand who else benefits from their efforts. Identifying the beneficiary group doesn't describe the form of the benefit,[3] but it has an impact on the decision for a prospective member to get involved. Table 4.1 shows that members can contribute their efforts to a number of possible beneficiaries.

TABLE 4.1   Potential Beneficiaries of Tasks

Beneficiary	Description
Task participant	Only members who participate in the task reap the results.
Social instance member	These are some or all members of a single instance of a social environment (for example, one person's social network, a single group, or a community), regardless of whether they participate in the task.
Ecosystem member	This includes anyone registered with the ecosystem—a collection of many social environment instances, such as many individuals, personal networks, groups, communities, and so on—regardless of whether they participate in the task.
Sponsor	This is the sponsor (individual or organization) that provides or supports the social system.

[3] It isn't always possible or desirable to ascribe value to the benefits or results of a social task, but take a look at Chapter 10, "Measuring Social Environments," for ideas on measuring social systems.

TABLE 4.1   Potential Beneficiaries of Tasks

Beneficiary	Description
Sponsor offering	In addition to the sponsor, members can potentially benefit as customers of these products, services, or other offerings.
Third party	The task benefits specific individuals or groups in addition to the members or the sponsor.
Anyone	This includes anyone in the domain, regardless of whether they are a member or whether they participate in the task.
Cause	This beneficiary is an altruistic or abstract cause or philosophy, such as averting poverty worldwide, aiming for a healthier workforce, or supporting environmental causes. These beneficiaries aim for wide categories of common interests instead of targeting specific populations or organizations.

Describing the Form of Aggregation

The next step of defining a social task is to consider how members perform this task collectively. Social software aggregates the behavior or content from many individuals into overall results or collections of results. However, you can use different methods to perform aggregation:

- **Independent**—Members work on the task separately, but the results are aggregated across all members. Their discrete actions and results might not be directly visible to others—the results are visible only a converged aggregate value (for example, closed ballot voting).

- **Autonomous**—Members work on the task separately of each other, and their results are distinctly visible to other members as separate work. This creates opportunities in which members might benefit from information that multiple other members share. A collection of divergent results across the many members or a single convergent result (such as brainstorming on ideas) can occur.

- **Consensus**—A group of members works directly together on the task with the *intent* to deliver an overall collective result, even if it's not unanimous or convergent. Tasks often require analysis, discussion, and debate to arrive at a collective answer. The ultimate goal is to converge and deliver a single collective result, but members might not always agree on one answer and there sometimes produce multiple options as results.

- **Deliberative**—A group of members works directly together without the intent or necessity of coming to a consensus on a single result. These are typically discussions or interactions that can spread out in many directions, depending on how subsets of members interact.

- **Combative**—Members must compete against each other to derive the best result from the group, denying other choices.[4] Unlike consensus forming, only a single answer is provided from all the choices the group generated.

Building a Template for a Task

Putting these methods together with the concepts covered previously, Table 4.2 illustrates a template we can build for these tasks. It identifies who could benefit from a task, the type of aggregation performed, social experience models that sites often apply to this task, and possible social leadership models.

TABLE 4.2   A Template for Social Tasks

Task
Beneficiaries
Aggregation
Experience
Leadership

Different Models of Social Tasks

Using this template approach, we can build models of various social tasks to apply to a social environment. Each of these tasks requires the necessary software implementations for members to

---

[4] Bryce Glass, *Designing Your Reputation System in 10! Easy Steps*, IA Summit 2008, Miami, Florida.

conduct the steps of the task. However, the focus is to differentiate between social tasks; understand the necessary settings for social experience, leadership, and aggregation models; and define the types of actions that occur in each task.

Idea Generation

Idea generation as a social task aims to use the energy of the social group to either develop or pick new ideas from many possible options. Because members can contribute many ideas at a time, these tasks often include methods to examine the top ideas. This type of social filtering is another social task that can work independently of idea generation, which Chapter 5, "Social Tasks: Creating and Managing Information," covers in more detail. In generating ideas, people have an advantage over computers because they can apply their experience, knowledge, brainpower, and inspiration to come up with a wide variety of options. The two common forms of social idea generation are *social brainstorming* and *prediction markets*.

Social Brainstorming

Social brainstorming creates an open stage for members to identify, discuss, and lobby for ideas. It can be open to any set of topics, but typically the sponsor sets a frame of reference. For example, IBM has been using social brainstorming in its Jam sessions since 2001. In 2006, its InnovationJam[5] drew more than 150,000 employees, partners, and family members to contribute on the themes of "Going Places," "Staying Healthy," "A Better Planet," and "Finance and

---

[5] Osvald M. Bjelland and Robert Chapman Wood, "An Inside View of IBM's InnovationJam," *MIT Sloan Management Review* (Fall 2008), Vol 50, No 1: 32–40. IBM's Jam sessions (see www.collaborationjam.com) are annual activities on a public-facing social site that enable employees, partners, and other members of the public to participate in a mass social brainstorm to address worldwide issues. Also see "IBM Jams: Big Blue Can Innovate, Too," by Robert Katz, on his WorldChanging blog, accessible at www.worldchanging. com/archives/005342.html; and see Martin LaMonica's article "IBM's Chief Steps into 'Second Life' for Incubator Launch," *ZDNet News* (14 November 2006), accessible at http://news.zdnet.com/2100-9595_22-150263.html.

Commerce." Other examples include Dell's IdeaStorm[6] and MZinga's IdeaShare for the "We Are Greater than Me" project.

These are open feedback platforms that can generate basic ideas and enable others to agree, disagree, or further develop the ideas. The sponsoring organization should provide some degree of commitment to turn the best ideas into real implementations or products. For example, IBM committed a $100 million fund to support the best ideas that its 2006 social brainstorming session produced. This eventually led to the creation of a number of new business activities for the company, covering ideas such as smart healthcare payment systems, real-time language-translation services, and the 3D Internet initiative.[7] More than just the carrot at the end, these social brainstorms also require leaders to champion the ideas, present them to others, or recruit others to help develop them. Otherwise, these ideas can die on the vine from inadequate support.

Although the mass collaboration model applies well when the only catalytic factor is the aggregate vote on each idea, a better experience model is a community formed around the topic with defined leaders in catalyst roles. Group collaboration might also work for smaller, more population-limited engagements.

Social brainstorming (see Table 4.3) can work with a defined group, community, or mass collaboration experience model. However, a community manager or catalyst must sponsor, promote, and support the idea to develop it from concept to reality. To accomplish this, social brainstorming can lead to *codevelopment* (covered later in this chapter). Ideally, many catalysts help ideas compete against each other for the most support. A delegated, representative, or starfish social leadership model can work well after the initial task of voting on ideas has taken place.

---

[6] Jeremiah Owyang, "When the Web Team Leads Product Development, the Evolution of Dell Hell to Dell Swell," Web Strategy Show, accessible at http://tinyurl.com/292qm9. This is a nice video interview between Owyang and Lionel Menchaca, blog strategist and community manager at Dell, with some discussion about IdeaStorm. The site itself is at www.dellideastorm.com.

[7] See note 5.

TABLE 4.3   Social Brainstorming as a Social Task

Task	Social brainstorming
Beneficiaries	Any
Aggregation	Autonomous, then consensus or combative
Experience	Closed or visible workgroups, community, or mass collaboration
Leadership	Delegated, representative, or starfish

Prediction Markets

An alternative to the free associative thinking approach of social brainstorming is the prediction market. A prediction market is typically a voting or speculation platform in which members can distribute a limited set of points across multiple ideas. Unlike social brainstorming, this task model involves a limited, although possibly numerous, predefined set of choices for ideas and a definite end date. Each session typically applies a single question to decide among multiple open-ended choices or possibilities—for example, "How many items of product X will we sell in the winter?" The value of assets can go up or down relative to each other until the end date, at which point you can examine the final status. This helps filter the most valued ideas to the top.

Best Buy's internal prediction market, called TagTrade,[8] enables its employees to speculate on a wide variety of business predictions (such as predicting revenue on Memorial Day or gift card sales on Father's Day) and also provides pure entertainment for employees (for example, predicting whether *Pirates of the Caribbean 3* would do better than *Spiderman 3* before the launch of each). The Hollywood Stock Exchange[9] is another example of members speculating on the potential box office success for new movies in the United States.

---

[8] Dawn Keller, *TagTrade: Best Buy's Prediction Market*, Prediction Markets Conference, Kansas City, Mo. (November 2007).

[9] Hollywood Stock Exchange, *Welcome to Hollywood Stock Exchange: The Entertainment Market*, (December 2008). Available online at www.hsx.com/about/whatishsx.htm.

The structured nature of a prediction market (see Table 4.4) suggests that mass collaboration is best suited to running the actual overall task. However, as the Hollywood Stock Exchange site shows, each asset or stock can also have an associated subcommunity within the overall ecosystem. This enables users to share views and often try to justify or negotiate their valuation in a shared context. Prediction markets pair mass collaboration with swarm leadership, and many possible communities with starfish leadership.

TABLE 4.4   A Prediction Market as a Social Task

Task	Prediction market
Beneficiaries	Any
Aggregation	Consensus
Experience	Mass collaboration, optionally with subcommunities or groups for discussions
Leadership	Swarm, with subgroups as starfish

Codevelopment

Codevelopment involves applying collective effort to transform an idea from a high-level concept into well-refined ideas or substance. Social brainstorming and predictive markets define what the social group considers interesting to pursue. Codevelopment can take the interesting ideas from social brainstorming and predictive markets to the next step of making them real. The outcomes can be products, services, knowledge, or other concrete ideas. Table 4.5 illustrates the spectrum of idea conception, development, and realization tasks, in which the "products" of social brainstorming and prediction markets are ideas. This section analyzes approaches for idea development realization: *crowdsourcing by template* or *auctions, distributed human computation*, and the development approach that originated from *open source development*.

TABLE 4.5   Different Models for Social Codevelopment

Type	What Is the Task's Focus	Who Creates Ideas	Who Develops Actual Product	Which Experience Model
Crowdsourcing by template (such as BurdaStyle)	Templates are offered for users to cocreate their own custom versions or designs of products.	The site provides tools or templates for membership to create new ideas and vote on the best ideas.	Members develop the product that might be handed to a dedicated product team for final implementation or packaging.	Mass collaboration.
Crowdsourcing by auctions (such as Inno-Centive.com)	Topics or problems are narrowly predefined.	A sponsor offers a specific problem to solve, possibly with an offered reward.	Members bid by auction to solve the problem in part or in full.	Mass collaboration.
Distributed human computation	Tasks can be deconstructed and completed in pieces.	Sponsors, leaders, or external customers pose computational tasks.	Members complete pieces of the problem and return to the site, which reassembles it into a complete result.	Mass collaboration.
Open source development (such as Mozilla)	The project has defined goals, but ongoing development can evolve the goals.	The membership defines the goals with help from leaders.	The community develops the product collectively.	Mass collaboration, defined groups, or community.

Crowdsourcing

Crowdsourcing has been one of the more pleasantly surprising outcomes of social computing. The idea poses a problem to a crowd of users that is impractical to solve through computation but is possible through human analysis. This is precisely the business model that InnoCentive.com and BurdaStyle have successfully discovered. Crowdsourcing works through a template-based approach that members can customize to create original designs, and also through an auction in which members bid to provide solutions to sponsors' or customers' projects.

Template-based crowdsourcing (or *socially-driven prototyping*— see Table 4.6) is handy when the problem can be defined in an easily understandable and reconfigurable way, but it requires human ingenuity to develop new designs or prototypes. BurdaStyle enables users to take virtual raw materials and create new designs or templates of their own with the help of online design tools, which other users then rate on their appeal.[10] This approach provides a mechanism to explore new designs and ideas with the help of consumers. It also helps promote greater use of products and drives revenue.

TABLE 4.6 Crowdsourcing by Template as a Social Task

Task	Crowdsourcing by template
Beneficiaries	Task participant, sponsor offering, ecosystem members, third parties, or anyone
Aggregation	Autonomous creation, deliberative or combative selection
Experience	Community and mass collaboration
Leadership	Centralized design and review steps, swarm acceptance steps

Crowdsourcing by auctions (or *idea outsourcing*) is better suited when it's difficult to define the subcomponents or steps needed to complete the task, and when the ingenuity of the social group is required to offer viable solutions. The sponsoring organization either puts a proposal out to bid with a given reward or asks bidders to provide their price.

Both crowdsourcing models work well in mass-collaborative experiences because participants work on an individual level according to their own motivations to provide part of the overall solution. The social group can be involved in the decision-making or voting processes for the best ideas (or can even use a prediction market).

---

[10] BurdaStyle is a project cofounded by Nora Abousteit and Benedikta von Karaisl of German publishing house Hubert Burda Media. Available online at www.burdastyle.com/content/about_us.

Distributed Human Computation

Amazon.com's Mechanical Turk[11]—a marketplace for piece-work that requires human intelligence—transforms an old idea in software computation into a social task: breaking down a computational problem into smaller pieces and spreading the piece-work over many "processors" to solve in parallel. This kind of parallel processing works best when one or more steps can be independently repeated over many subsets. The social task version, which replaces computer processors with people, works well for tasks that computers find difficult to analyze yet can be fairly straightforward for the human brain. For example, identifying some object or recognizing specific people in a photo requires an understanding of what constitutes the boundaries between objects, knowing how to interpret objects from different angles, and recognizing an object from a lifetime of memories. Each participant performs this action on a single photo, repeated many times for a whole collection of photos. By working in parallel, people can find commonalities more quickly than it would take a computer system to analyze these photos. Amazon offers this business service to customers with such problems to analyze, and then handles how the work is broken down and assigned to members in this social environment. Amazon's service then consolidates the results and returns them to the customer.

Although this is "distributed computing," because the problem set can be broken down into units that many computation units (people) can process in parallel, the key point is that the human mind is doing the processing, not computers. The process also differs from the other forms of crowdsourcing by template and auction because each member doesn't take on a unique project of his or her own, and it might not involve as much creative thinking or originality (see Table 4.7).

Open Source Development

Open source development can be more effective than other varieties of codevelopment in creating the detailed implementations of projects. Members can be involved in this task on many levels, from working on small improvements independently of the main effort, to

---

[11] Amazon.com, *Mechanical Turk* available online at www.amazon.com/gp/help/customer/display.html/ref=hp_navbox_lnbus_turk?nodeId=16465291.

TABLE 4.7   Distribution of Human Computation as a Social Task

Task	Distributed human computation
Beneficiaries	Sponsor, sponsor offering, task participants, third party, or causes
Aggregation	Independent
Experience	Mass collaboration, supporting community
Leadership	Computation as a swarm; delegated, representative, or starfish supporting community

taking on a deep-level involvement in designing, implementing, and leading the project. They also generally have a lot of freedom in how to carry out the task. Open source development stems from software-development projects in which the software source code is available and visible to any potential developers who want to improve it. This contrasts with the "closed" approach of many software vendors who closely guard access to their software and limit anyone but their own developers from making any changes.

Open source development can work in a defined group, a community, or a mass collaboration (see Table 4.8). It's possible to carry out such a development in multiple parallel experiences:

- A defined group of members who know each other well and handle the core development effort
- A community that exchanges ideas and helps improve the components
- Members who create improvements or additions just for themselves, which they eventually give back to the project—essentially acting as a mass collaboration

TABLE 4.8   Public Open Source Project Development as a Task

Task	Public open source projects
Beneficiaries	Anyone—ecosystem or instance members, causes, or sponsor offerings
Aggregation	Autonomous contributions, and consensus or combative on final choices
Experience	Primarily community, secondary groups, and mass collaborations
Leadership	Primarily delegated, representative, or starfish leadership

Finding People

Social computing tools are a great way to locate people, either by proactively seeking out people or by serendipitously finding them in a location. As with other social tools, having a social environment with an active and well-identified population is more likely to help someone find a good match. Although successfully finding exactly who you are looking for depends on the list of members in the social environment, you should consider how this task works independently of the chances of success. Some tools also discover and map the relationships between people based on content in enterprise databases and e-mail systems.

Relationship Mapping and Mining

Managing and discovering contacts comes naturally to a system that focuses on the social interactions of many users. Keeping track of contacts is an essential part of business. However, traditional contact-management systems and relationship databases that require users to actively submit the status of contacts and relationships can quickly become outdated and require too much time to maintain manually.

However, social computing tools can develop an almost real-time perspective of relationships as a constantly changing and evolving model. Tools such as BranchIt Corporation's eponymous software and IBM Lotus Atlas for Connections can examine the interactions between users as they occur and map the relationships. These tools examine social interactions in different channels such as e-mail, instant messaging, enterprise databases, and other tools that embody shared or social activities among a known set of users who have given their permission. In essence, a relationship-mapping tool creates a collection of social networks across all these users. Users might be able to see only their own networks, but these applications could help users also discover other connections through their intermediary relationships (see Table 4.9). Although users might recognize many of the people in their networks, they might also be surprised at the new possibilities such systems discover or might see relationships they didn't know they had.

TABLE 4.9   Relationship Mapping and Mining as a Social Task

Task	Relationship mapping and mining
Beneficiaries	Task participants or social instance members
Aggregation	Autonomous
Experience	Social network and community
Leadership	Centralized

Location-Centered Social Interactions

When people share information on their current or planned future location, it creates opportunities where people can meet each other, learn from their shared expertise, or state their opinions and preferences. This can be particularly useful for meeting new people at business events such as trade shows and conferences, or for locating peers and experts (see Table 4.10).

TABLE 4.10   Location-Centered Interactions as a Social Task

Task	Location-centered social interactions
Beneficiaries	Task participant, social instance members, or ecosystem members
Aggregation	Autonomous
Experience	Social network or individual
Leadership	Centralized

The Dopplr social site provides ways for members to share their upcoming travel destination or information with others, either privately to their social network or openly to any other member of the site.[12] Dopplr users identify a city or location and dates when they will be going. As they travel, they might find other users in their social network in the vicinity, or vice versa. Other users watching them can be notified of their plans, saving them from needing to recall or find people in each location to notify them of their plans.

---

[12] Dopplr is a social atlas service for travelers to share travel plans and patterns among people, founded by Marko Athisaari (Finland) and Matt Biddulph (UK). Available online at www.dopplr.com/main/about.

This also creates serendipitous opportunities to meet others if, for example, they happen to be in the same city at the same time. Although Dopplr itself is nonspecific in its use, many possible scenarios arise. Researchers and academics can use it to discover opportunities to meet their peers at different events. Consultants can use it to discover which knowledge experts are available in their region. On a personal level, enterprising parents can use it to set up play dates for their children.

BrightKite is another tool to help people discover each other based on geolocation, especially through cellphones.[13] This site enables users to share their location information and status autonomously (per the description in the earlier section "Form of Aggregation") with others in the social network they identify, or share it openly with everyone to meet new people. These tools do allow for privacy. For example, BrightKite can limit who can see a user's location and can also limit this to a certain physical range (up to 500 meters) based on the member's availability or privacy indicator.

Summary

Performing work collectively as a social group involves more than just gathering people in a virtual place. It involves the social group at some point of the task—in input, analysis, or output—aggregating the work through one of several ways. The work to perform, the social task, frequently recurs in common patterns across many social environments. By creating a model for a social task, you can consider the situation necessary to enable group work based on the social experience model, the government, the aggregation approach, and the interpersonal, content, or environment actions involved.

The different task models described in this chapter focus on ways people can collaborate in pairs, small groups, or large populations. Chapter 5 further explains how to work with information in social task models.

---

[13] Brady Becker, "New Features: Place Privacy and People Near Me," BrightKite Blog (July 2008). Accessible at http://blog.brightkite.com/2008/07/30/new-features-place-privacy-people-near-me/.

5

Social Tasks: Creating and Managing Information

Working with information that is unstructured or qualitatively subjective is another category of tasks that can be complex for software to solve by itself. Often such information requires a human perspective to indicate preference, quote alternative sources, categorize, or filter to add perspective, supporting material, or assessment of quality. This helps others consider, consume, or apply this information to their own work. Social computing tasks help guide a group to analyze information in this way. By simplifying the steps and working with crowds, it is possible to build substantial information about any subject. This chapter examines three categories of social tasks involved in creating or managing information: recommendations and reviews, creating and categorizing, and information filtering.

Recommendations and Reviews

Social computing embraces and enhances the natural inclination of many people to offer their opinion on practically any subject they care to talk about.[1] This is evident not only in the many variations of ratings, reviews, and recommendations found on sites, but also in the marketing tactics companies use to promote by word-of-mouth.

---

[1] This is culture dependent. Some cultures don't encourage directly offering contrarian opinions or ideas to their seniors or managers. In such cultures, social users often take on pseudonyms or aliases to enable them to contribute but not interfere with the cultural norms.

Reviews

Online qualitative review systems enable social environments to collect user opinions in different ways. Analysts have researched review systems and the influence of reviews[2] on products and services. How is this different in the online environment? The statistical processes for analyzing quantitative ratings remain the same, although collection, storage, and processing have become easier. However, creating a balanced system for qualitative reviews continues to be an art form, even on online systems.

What has changed is the distribution of this information, and integration into other systems. Regardless of the domain of the system, it has become much easier to refer to particular ratings and items and to redistribute these opinions to others. Digg.com's metric (the number of "diggs") refers to how many individuals have indicated that a news item on some Web site is worth others' consideration. Other sites can also depict this rating as a widget, showing the value of the content item on an industry-wide scale (digg.com). Review systems providers such as Bazaarvoice and PowerReviews offer a service that organizations can add to their own sites in the public-facing domain. People can also apply the survey tools discussed in Chapter 10, "Measuring Social Environments," to gather ratings and reviews in other domains.

In product reviews, the reviewer's identity assuages bias. Knowing that the reviewer has actually purchased the product also matters. Amazon.com's RealName system[3] is intended to provide assurance of users' identities by authenticating them based on their credit card information. PowerReviews's Verified Buyer[4] program verifies that reviewers have actually purchased the product they are discussing. Both programs lend credibility and reputation to reviewers.

---

[2] Grant Blank, *Critics, Ratings, and Society: The Sociology of Ratings* (Lanham, Maryland: Rowman & Littlefield, 2006). Blank covers a wide range of research about reviews and ratings systems.

[3] Amazon.com, *Your Real Name Attribution* (August 2008). Available online at www.amazon.com/gp/help/customer/display.html?nodeId=14279641.

[4] PowerReviews, PowerReviews Customer Reviews Service (July 2008). Available online at www.powerreviews.com/social-shopping/solutions/customer-reviews.html.

Quantitative ratings are typically consensus focused, whereas qualitative reviews consolidate many autonomous or combative individual reviews. Reviews can be quite descriptive and can be considered content items in their own right if they are substantial and useful to the social group. Reviews can drive some discussion and deliberation as a community experience (see Table 5.1). To gather more users or customers, companies can use reviews and ratings as recommendations to distribute socially.

TABLE 5.1   Reviews as a Social Task

Task	Reviews
Beneficiaries	Any
Aggregation	Autonomous, deliberative, or combative
Experience	Individual or community
Leadership	Centralized or starfish

Direct Social Recommendations

After users create or discover some piece of content, a common instinct is to (positively or negatively) recommend it to others they know. Unlike reviews, which are open to anyone else in the domain, direct social recommendations emphasize direct relationships. Therefore, reviews can easily be a feature of social network and defined group experiences. This form of word-of-mouth transmission of recommendations directly among users has several possible mechanisms.

One approach is to formalize word-of-mouth as a marketing campaign. A company can operate a word-of-mouth program in many ways, incorporating features such as tracking paths across users, collecting sales leads, and even rewarding participants. The Word-of-Mouth Marketing Association lists numerous business providers that can assist others in conducting such a campaign.[5]

Even without such a formalized program, basic systems simply entice users to e-mail a friend about a site they have seen. This

---

[5] WOMMA.org, WOMMA Member Directory (September 2008). Accessible at www.womma.org/members/.

information can be fed to a social navigation system that shows "most e-mailed pages." The site typically automatically generates a formatted e-mail in which the sender identifies himself and one or more addresses. The generated e-mail might have a Web URL with special parameters to identify it as an invitation from another user. This helps the site measure the success rate of invitations. Beyond this "e-mail a friend" system, other word-of-mouth methods frequently use a standard URL with a special parameter or tag. A word-of-mouth marketing program might invite a core set of members to formally sign up to participate to receive marketing messages (containing a tagged URL) and, by their own means, distribute these messages to others they know (their social network).

The converse of pushing recommendations to people is when users intentionally want to receive (or pull) notifications from others (see Table 5.2). This pull for information is common when a member is trying to keep up with the activities of their friends, peers, or managers. For example, the Flock browser enables people to invite peers to participate in a particular group so that each member can share with the group Web locations, images, audio, video, or other items they find interesting. Members still control their own browsers, but they can receive a stream of suggestions from fellow group members in the browser.

TABLE 5.2   Direct Social Recommendation as a Social Task

Task	Direct social recommendations by notification
Beneficiaries	Task participants, social instance members, and sponsor offerings
Aggregation	Autonomous
Experience	Individual and social network
Leadership	Centralized

Microblogging social tools such as Twitter, Plurk, and Identi.ca enable members to share their activities or interests with peers, or follow other members. Members can post a short paragraph of text (typically 140 words or less) that is automatically distributed to all those who are following them. This enables both the push and pull models of direct social recommendations. As with individual blogs, authors share their ideas and suggestions with others in an individual experience, often to build a reputation for themselves as a useful resource. Companies are also actively present in these ecosystems of users to share their content and communicate with or respond to users. For example, the Scottsdale, Arizona, police department uses Twitter to send urgent notifications to any followers on their computers or cellphones.[6] Similarly, NASA actively shares information with the public about the ongoing activities of the Mars Phoenix Lander spacecraft.[7]

Derived Social Recommendations

Some social systems can process the behavior of a social group over time and generate recommendations based on this data. The input is still social, derived from the natural behavior of many users on the site. However, complex software analysis generated the recommendations instead of direct content suggestions from other users (see Table 5.3). Unlike the direct recommendation approach, the visibility of other users or their choices is not an important factor to newly arrived users.

TABLE 5.3   Derived Social Recommendation as a Social Task

Task	Derived social recommendation
Beneficiaries	Task participants
Aggregation	Independent or consensus for contributors
Experience	Personal for task user Community or mass collaboration for contributors
Leadership	Centralized per task user Representative, starfish, or swarm for contributors

The Netflix online movie rental store has a renowned recommendation system that offers suggestions that pair members' movie

6 Amanda Keim, "Scottsdale Police Twitter to Get the Word Out," *The East Valley Tribune* (online) (Scottsdale, Ariz.: 5 September 2008). Accessible at www.eastvalleytribune.com/story/124996.

7 Alan Boyle, "Mars Lander Is a Web Star," MSNBC.com (30 May 2008). Accessible at http://cosmiclog.msnbc.msn.com/archive/2008/05/30/1085295.aspx.

interests with models of what they and other members have chosen, as aggregated from the combined social behavior. The algorithm is confidential, but the business value as a competitive advantage is evident; this recommendation system trumps the classic model promoted in movie stores that offer picks by their employees, their own experts, or well-known movie reviewers.

In a different version of this idea, MarketWatch.com provides a portlet of information that highlights Most Read and Most Commented content items. Other sites offer the Most Emailed category. Each of these traffic-relevant methods points out aggregate social behavior to offer suggestions that might interest other users.

Information visualization plays a strong role in this task by showing different ways of linking pieces of information or knowledge, showing priority items, or providing filtering options. These navigation elements might appear in these formats:

- **Sorted list**—Placing the terms in some form of sorting order, such as alphabetically or by date, relevancy, or other sort options.

- **Tag cloud**—The terms are positioned near each other as if floating in a cloud, with significant terms enhanced in bigger fonts or brighter colors.

- **Treemap**—Each term has a set of boxes, decreasing in size from the top term to the lowest term. The name derives from a software programming data structure called a tree, which is then mapped to a visual model as boxes.

- **Network diagram**—This is similar to a tag cloud, but with a web of connections between related terms.

- **Sliding filter**—This format sets a threshold, showing fewer terms or more terms, beginning with the top terms.

Creating and Categorizing Information

Social tools often provide a common means of creating content in a freeform manner, as users see fit. The task of creating information overlaps with other tasks, such as gathering resources and defining categories, making them difficult to separate. Therefore, all these tasks are similar types.

Sharing Collections

Creating a list of information is one of the simplest approaches to categorizing information. Sharing a collection or a list is a natural outgrowth of the social Web. By sharing a list they created, users are essentially lending their opinion and credibility to the contents, and vice versa. A list is a simple suggestion of how a user categorizes a particular selection of information. This task focuses on the collection-creation process instead of the recommendation action (see Table 5.4).

TABLE 5.4   Sharing Collections as a Social Task

Task	Sharing collections
Beneficiaries	Any
Aggregation	Autonomous, deliberative, and combative
Experience	Individual and community
Leadership	Centralized and starfish

Online shopping sites today have ways to save the current virtual shopping cart of items that a customer might want. However, not all sites enable users to share these lists with others; their lists simply enable users to delay purchase for a later time without needing to find all the items when they return in the future—the lists foster a personal experience.

In contrast, when a shopper wants to share a wish list of items with friends, this changes the list to an individual or social network experience and requires mechanisms for other users to manage purchases from that user's list. This is essentially the same idea as a gift registry (for a wedding, a birthday, or some other event).

A shared list is also a process of recommending or categorizing items. For example, I share my list of social computing books on Amazon.com's Listmania, with a short description of my views on each.[8] I use it as a way to quickly recall what I thought of each book,

---

[8] Rawn Shah, *My Social Networking Book List*. Accessible at Rawn Shah's developerWorks space, at http://tinyurl.com/6noq72.

but others might see it as a recommendation on useful books on this particular topic. Because this list is on a public ecosystem of other shared lists, it is my individual experience instance. All these varieties focus on a centralized leadership approach to creating a collection of information.

Folksonomies and Social Tagging

Social bookmarking expanded the idea of storing bookmarks on a Web browser to storing them on another Web site so that other browsers and people can access them. Adding *tags* to each bookmark enables users to create their own index to find information according to their individual preference. *Social tagging* combines the entries from many users under each tag into a common set. You can apply this tagging technology to any kind of information by a group (social tagging in general), not just Web bookmarks (social bookmarking).

This technology combines information from many people to create a richer set of information about any subject. The overlap of different mental indexes from many people helps identify common interests and common cross-references, while also adding different possible sources of information. Most systems also eschew qualifying or weighing the quality of such content in favor of creating a simple yet dynamic, evolving system.

This is an entirely different approach to structuring information (see Table 5.5) than top-down approaches of a core team of people creating a hierarchical or networked taxonomy (such as mapping a family tree or a network of friends) or organizing information by aspect (such as organizing music by genres). It is freeform and driven from the bottom up by many users acting independently and shaping it by virtue of their shared social environments—it truly deserves a new name: *folksonomy*.

TABLE 5.5 A Folksonomy as a Social Task

Task	Folksonomy
Beneficiaries	Any
Aggregation	Deliberative and autonomous
Experience	Mass collaboration
Leadership	Swarm

Social bookmarking in folksonomies, such as the social tool sites del.icio.us, stumbleupon, dogear, and reddit, popularized this concept by focusing on two common needs: the need to share Web links with others and the need for a better way to store and categorize one's Web bookmarks beyond a single computer. Such sites overcome the undesirable side effects of the information-intensive world: information locked into an individual's head or a local machine, and conflicts over how information should be categorized. No single team or software approach finds and categorizes this information—the strength of many human minds indexes and shares the information with others.

The Enterprise Tagging Service on IBM's worldwide intranet provides a social tagging alternative to traditional search engines to make enterprise information easier to find across the company. IBM worldwide intranet users can tag information according to how they would individually describe it, find tags they contributed, find others who used the same tag, and find other relevant resources associated with the tag. This helps users navigate in several ways and saves the company an estimated $7.5 million in productivity improvements, in addition to the value of the information.[9] A folksonomy can avoid the classic problems of *groupthink*—in which a small group of people who frequently work together develop similar or unilateral ways of looking at information, limiting innovation and new ideas—by removing the need to directly negotiate common meaning or categorization, or by inviting others beyond the group to participate in the information categorization.

IBM Lotus Connections software enables users to socially tag people in the system in addition to any content. This reshapes the purpose and the results of social tagging to focus on individual characterstics and skills. Users can add tags to describe themselves or others. This can help the user find others by, for example, their skill set, product or technology focus, or even personal interests. Although users follow their own approach to define tags for people, the combined social effect groups other people with similar skills or other

---

[9] CIO Magazine Editors, "2008 Winner Profile: IBM," *CIO Magazine* (online). Accessible at www.cio.com/cio100/detail/1840.

tags. Therefore, this process becomes a way to find other people or their skills through social tagging.

Social tagging is becoming an underlying infrastructure element of many group-oriented tools, such as wikis, forums, and content databases, as a way for members to create an aggregate index of the information. In fact, this is where *social* tagging is sometimes confused with nonsocial tagging (or simply, tagging). For example, an individual (using the centralized or delegated leadership models) blogger can create tags for each content item they post. Even when there are a few contributors to the blog, this tagging is not on par with a folksonomy (which uses a swarm leadership model).

Both collection creation and social tagging tend to be structured forms of creating online content. Creating a collection to share with others involves adding specific items, typically a description, a location, and other particulars about the item. Social tagging and bookmarking usually involve a simple association: a tag to one or more Web locations, optionally with a short textual description.

Direct Social Content Creation

Creating freeform content is a more complex matter than applying the structured approach of social tagging. It can involve a number of subtasks: writing the content; formatting it; editing it; adding resources and relevant links; and adding subcategories, derivatives, and alternatives. It's difficult to say where one of these subtasks ends and another begins because users can choose whether to perform any of these tasks, and defining content is highly subjective. Therefore, these subtasks are simply lumped together as a single task here. Several users usually cooperate and manually create such content in a social environment (see Table 5.6), differentiating this process from a nonsocial task.

TABLE 5.6   Direct Social Content Creation as a Social Task

Task	Direct social content creation
Beneficiaries	Any
Aggregation	Consensus or deliberative
Experience	Individual, defined group, and community
Leadership	Centralized, delegated, representative, and starfish

Wikipedia, Google's Knol, and About.com are examples of a task to create a world of information socially. All these sites enable users to create any kind of information. Similarly, Wiktionary provides a free online dictionary of terms, and WikiQuote provides a collection of gathered quotes and sayings.

Some content items become categories in their own right when users start to break them up into multiple content items because of subvarieties, alternatives, and derivates from the original content. The capability to maintain and manage multiple versions of a single content item, as in wikis, typically still results in one final product.

Mahalo is a search engine powered by people and is a social group that finds, collects, analyzes, and populates information on any given term. Mahalo seeks out popular terms that users search for and actively contributes content under these terms. Unlike the social tagging approach of folksonomies to which a wide population can contribute, only Mahalo's employees screen and filter these terms. Users can then search on these terms and responses.[10] The manual process might mean fewer answers, but that isn't necessarily a bad thing: A search conducted on major search engines such as Google, MSN, or Yahoo! can result in hundreds of thousands of responses, which mostly go ignored in favor of the top entries.

Derived Social Content Generation

Other tools derive and format content from a variety of sources and users, similar to the way some social tools derive social recommendations through software analysis. For example, profile generators can search popular social sites or search engines to discover publicly available information about a particular person. In a way, search engines themselves derive content from the network of links that many users create (see Table 5.7).

Zoominfo.com is an automated profile generator that searches the Internet for information on any entered name and tries to assemble a profile about that person by combining all these sources. Although this

---

[10] Adam L. Penenberg, "Man vs. Machine," FastCompany.com (September 2007). Accessible at www.fastcompany.com/magazine/118/man-vs-machine.html.

TABLE 5.7   Derived Social Content Creation as a Social Task

Task	Derived social content creation
Beneficiaries	Any
Aggregation	Consensus and deliberative
Experience	Individual and community
Leadership	Centralized

is an automated process, it creates an individual experience instance about anyone who is visible. A person can claim the profile by creating an identity on the site after a verification process. A moral question arises about the significance of a system that can create a profile from information that is already public but is now gathered in one spot. However, it is an example of how an automated system can create a social instance.

Filtering Information

Many users seek out social sites with the objective of finding specific information they need from social groups or achieving some personal goal. This individually directed motive still relies on a social mechanism, even if the individual connects with only one other member in the social group to achieve it. Social benefit to others still can arise in some cases: A solution to one user's problem could be helpful for other users.

In a Web 1.0 view, social systems such as forums often had a document such as a frequently asked questions (FAQ) list created by experts and then shared with everyone. This task model still exists, but social software has progressed significantly so that the goal-seeking process is now more personalized and focused to each user's needs.

The different models for tasks in individual goal achievement include finding expert contacts; getting personalized advice, answers, or support; and finding information socially. Some sites implement a way for their individual goal-seeking model to reward the people who submit answers, such as the goal-seeker awarding points for help received, the social group weighing the responses and selecting the best one, or the site itself awarding points for the most popular or most referenced answers.

Social Q&A Systems

Instead of directly seeking individual experts from a social group, this social task gathers answers from potentially many sources and then enables users to pick from the possible choices. It doesn't guarantee quality or even a promise of getting any answers. However, these sites provide a way to access the minds of many people for a single goal (see Table 5.8). Success in this task model requires active participation by members. Some sites offer explicit rewards, and others focus on promoting the competence of the people who respond.

TABLE 5.8   A Social Q&A System as a Social Task

Task	Social Q&A systems
Beneficiaries	Task participants
Aggregation	Autonomous or deliberative
Experience	Community, social network, and mass collaboration
Leadership	Any type is possible, but it depends on the experience model

Many sites implement the community experience for this task, creating a place users can go to ask questions of a given community. Discussion forums have been used for this task for decades across generations of social tools, from Usenet newsgroups in the 1980s to the Web-based forums of today. Because of its long history, this could be the most popular use of social tools and task models; it frequently serves as the framework for a vendor's product support forums. Users post a question in a particular forum that appears relevant to what they're seeking and wait to get responses from other members; sometimes members provide multiple answers and argue the merits of one solution over another.

Users can also perform this task in a social network or as a mass collaboration experience. For example, LinkedIn enables members to solicit their specific social network for answers to any kind of question. However, users have no guarantee that they will get a useful answer, and their chances of success depend on whom they connect to. Yahoo! Answers is an example of a mass collaboration in which a user can pose a question to the entire population and enable other users to submit their own answers; the user then picks the best answer. Mobile Web tools like Chacha.com or KGB.com offer a similar activity as a personal experience: Users submit questions to the site through their cellphones,[11] and the social site distributes the questions to its group of experts who search, filter, and then deliver a response as a text message to the phone, for a small fee.

Summary

Although you can create and share content in a social environment in many forms, the separate tasks of creating content, making recommendations, and filtering this information define this process. Users can manually perform some of these tasks, such as creating content and making recommendations. On a parallel level, the software itself can provide the content or recommendations based on information gathered about a social group instead of direct input from users. The task of navigating information through the collective intelligence of a social group helps filter what other users find useful. These are all information tasks that can benefit the social group, combining individual responses and actions into socially validated results.

Much of the participation in such tasks depends on how people react to the culture of the social environment and experience, and how leaders encourage members to get involved. The next two chapters cover these topics.

---

[11] Chacha.com, *How It Works* (August 2008). Accessible at http://answers.chacha.com/?page_id=35.

6

Social Ecosystems and Domains

Many organizations combine multiple social experiences into one social environment. Some organizations also support multiple parallel environments with the same experience, leadership, and task model, but different content and membership. They can place these environments under a single leadership, or they can unite many distinct environments but still allow each its own leadership. By defining the target audience and domain each audience comes from, they can also create appropriate governance guidelines and shape the culture of the environments.

Consider the following approaches to grouping different combinations and collections of social experiences and environments:

- Grouping many instances
- Grouping multiple tools within a single instance
- Grouping audiences and supporting participants in different domains (employees, partners, existing customers, customer leads, and shareholders)

Grouping Instances

Some social systems enable many social environments—each generically referred to as an *instance*—to exist simultaneously in parallel. Each instance within this *ecosystem* can support a different purpose or a different set of users. A *homogenous ecosystem* of social environments has many instances; all have the same set of social tools but different owners, leaders, leadership approaches, or topics of focus. For example, the social site Wordpress.com provides a homogenous ecosystem of thousands of instances of blogs, each run by different bloggers for their own purposes, but all using the same base blogging application. Homogeneous ecosystems frequently enable each set of environment owners to customize their environment to help them differentiate themselves, or to promote their group culture or individual personality.

General Electric, Intel, and IBM run complex ecosystems of social computing environments internally for their employees. They provide directories to enable employees to understand the location, reporting structure, interests, or other social information that they share. The companies provide wikis that enable groups to record and share their knowledge on different subjects, thus reducing the chances of losing this knowledge when employees change focus or jobs; it also eliminates the need to reinvent the wheel in different pockets within the organization. IBM provides enterprise-wide instant messaging and Web conferencing to enable employees to communicate with each other across departments and organizational silos, and as a business alternative to long-distance phone calls across regions and countries. Laurie Buczek, Intel's global Web program manager, points to other needs for social computing in the enterprise, such as integrating new hires into a complex organization, learning through on-the-job training, and supporting organizational restructuring.[1]

The GE, Intel, and IBM examples are *heterogeneous ecosystems* of social environments that can support many different social tools and tasks, with different groupings and purposes for each. Heterogeneous ecosystems enable a greater variety of interaction and social tasks, but at the price of supporting a diverse set of applications and ways of using these tools.

The concept of *multitenancy* can go a step beyond the idea of ecosystems. A multitenant environment can support diverse groups, each within its own "walled garden"—visitors need to first enroll as members before they can see other users or the content within the garden. Because each walled garden is essentially isolated from the

---

[1] Laurie Buczek, "Why Intel Is Investing in Social Computing," IT@Intel Blog (13 February 2009). Available at http://communities.intel.com/openport/community/openportit/it/blog/2009/02/13/why-intel-is-investing-in-social-computing.

others, this approach is useful when social environments don't need to share the same identity, culture, or goals, or aren't part of the same organization. Multitenant systems can consist of many isolated instances in a single ecosystem, or can host multiple separate ecosystems.

A number of multitenancy systems exist, such as Ning.com and IBM LotusLive, which can provide entire ecosystems to each tenant. The LotusLive platform also enables tenants to open portions of their collaboration environment to partners (in other tenancies), enabling border crossings to work across organizational landscapes.

Grouping Tools

Social software applications can also provide many choices of tools to users in complex ecosystems and multitenant systems. For example, each IBM LotusLive tenant can implement services such as Web conference meetings, instant messaging, file sharing, tagging, searching for expertise across the group, and more.[2] However, each customer must consider how and where to apply these tools to complete different tasks. As described in Chapter 2, "Sharing a Social Experience," users can apply a single social tool in different contexts of experience, apply different leadership models (as described in Chapter 3, "Leadership in Social Environments"), and conduct different social tasks (as described in Chapter 4, "Social Tasks: Collaborating on Ideas," and Chapter 5, "Social Tasks: Creating and Managing Information"). The social environment owners must still decide how they want to apply the tools in their environment.

Although they can support multiple experiences across the tools, this kind of *multifunction* or *multitool* environment is still open to one overall set of members. Similar to a department store, such environments cater to different content, interests, and activities for all customers. Customers can choose to interact in the areas they find interesting. Sometimes this means that one area or one tool in the environment might be very popular but another might lack traffic.

---

[2] LotusLive is a software service or application service hosted on IBM's server environment and delivered to customers over the Internet. See www.lotuslive. com.

GoingOn.com offers a general-purpose multitool or multifunction platform for any customer, but it also packages solutions for particular industries or common group activities.[3] For example, its GO
Social Learning Platform solution for educational institutions focuses
on the particular social tools that students, teachers, and administra-
tors can use to connect and share ideas through discussion forums,
calendars, media galleries, collaboration workgroups, and more. Similarly, ProjectSpaces.com from Forum One Communications Corp. is
another multitool environment specifically aimed at collaborating
and managing projects.

The multitool scenario for GoingOn makes sense because each
solution has an overall purpose—such as helping students interact
and collaborate within educational institutions—and the various tools
within the package directly support the goals of this purpose. The
users share the same context for the purpose even while pursuing different activities, and they develop a shared sense of culture within the
environment.

Grouping Audiences into Domains

The next dimension of grouping examines the question of *where*
participants in a social environment come from. This is a concern in
many businesses, particularly in relation to who has access to the
information in the environment. Online social experiences all reside
on some shared computer system or network inside an organization
or in a public environment. Within a company, the social experience
might be available to all employees or perhaps just a select few. Outside an organization, the social experience might be available to anyone on the Internet, or it could be open to select partners with whom
members of the organization can collaborate.

A social *domain* describes the target audience to whom you offer
the social environment. Although all domains involve some type of

---

[3] GoingOn's GO Social Learning Platform provides a number of customizable
services for various types of educational communities, such as supporting educators alone or providing interaction between educators and students. See www.
goingon.com/GoingOn/products.html.

collaboration, the nature of the different audiences shown in Table 6.1 is important. The four types of domains shown here describe social environments within the enterprise, those visible to the public, those that span the organization's external boundary, and those that are available on third-party sites.

Table 6.1 shows the U.S. Air Force Knowledge Network as a private enterprise domain across a global network for U.S. Air Force personnel to develop internal communities on logistics and communicate across their globally distributed organization. Similarly, General Electric supports enterprise-wide social computing services through its SupportCentral to enable employees to create communities among practitioners focused in the same technology, skill set or industry (a community of practice) across the company.

TABLE 6.1   Types of Social Domains

Domain	Sponsors and Owners	Audience	Audience Collaboration Goals	Example
Enterprise	From one company	Members from the same company	Collaboration among employees	The U.S. Air Force Knowledge Network[4] and GE's internal SupportCentral.[5]
Public-facing	From one company	Members from a sponsoring organization and the public	Collaboration among people in sponsoring organization and public populations	The SAP Developer Network[6] provides social environments for its customers and the public interested in its products.
Cross-boundary	A primary sponsoring organization with secondary partners	Members from each organization	Collaboration among the sponsoring organization and partners or customers in invitation-only or limited-access environments	Companies using IBM LotusLive or GoingOn can hold separate Web conference sessions, or share content with each partner.

TABLE 6.1   Types of Social Domains

Domain	Sponsors and Owners	Audience	Audience Collaboration Goals	Example
Third-party	A sponsoring organization using or partnering with a third-party social ecosystem	Members from the third-party ecosystem	Members from the public or the existing population of a popular ecosystem who are invited to collaborate with the sponsor	Ernst & Young uses the social site Facebook as a recruiting ground for new employees and already has 11,000 employees on the site.[7]

SAP Developer Network, introduced in Chapter 1, "Social Software on the Ascent," serves an open public audience of IT personnel among customers and partners. Salespeople use IBM's LotusLive system to make presentations and interact with customer representatives during the course of a complex sales deal. General Motors also engages users on popular car-enthusiast social environments, such as Facebook and Edmunds.com, to gather diverse viewpoints, societal issues, and product interests from across the global marketplace to understand trends and market products. Ernst & Young encourages its employees to use Facebook as a strategic tool to draw new employees and export their own organizational culture.

Members from the same company are likely to share the same organizational cultural values and be familiar with some of the internal structure or workings of the company. In a cross-boundary situation, however, members from different organizations can have different behavioral norms and work cultures, with different goals and motivations. Similarly, social environment leaders would likely

---

[4] Randy Adkins, "The Air Force Knowledge Network," presented at the Enterprise/Mobile/Social Networking Conference 2008, San Francisco (10 July 2008).

[5] Sukh Garewal, GE's *SupportCentral Collaboration and Workflow Environment*, Office 2.0 Conference, San Francisco (September 2008).

[6] For more information about the SAP Developer Network, see Chapter 2.

[7] H. Green, "The Water Cooler Is Now on the Web," BusinessWeek.com (1 October 2007). Accessible at www.businessweek.com/print/magazine/content/07_40/b4052072.htm?chan=mz.

work differently with a group of employees from their own organization than with business partners or customers.

Organizations aren't limited to just one of these environments. For example, thousands of employees collaborate with each other across the IBM global intranet: They work with partners through LotusLive, Partnerworld, and other services. They also interact with developers, customers, and industry specialists through the IBM developerWorks ecosystem. IBM even reaches out to alumni and potential new hires through social networks such as Xing, LinkedIn, and Facebook.

Aaron Strout, a social media expert, suggests that you might want to take both approaches: joining a third-party site in addition to having a social instance of your own.[8] In particular, some customers might already be on third-party sites, and this lowers the barrier for them to join your activities.

Domain boundaries identify demarcation points in which governance issues, such as acceptable behavior policies and usage guidelines, can come into play. Some organizations develop policies and guidelines for the entire domain that might have an impact on any social experience within. This helps set the tone and make it simpler for individual organizations or teams within that domain to create their own experiences.

Who in the Organization Should Run the Social Environment?

Although the social domain needs to be accessible by the intended target audience, this isn't necessarily an indication of where the software exists—which is important for enterprise IT resource planning and sometimes to the access and information security level as well. Often larger organizations can have several social computing efforts running in different departments. This particularly has an impact on the question of authority across the environment. This

---

[8] Aaron Strout and Jennifer Leggio, "Enterprise Communities: Build or Join?" ZDNet News & Blogs: Jennifer Leggio (23 July 23 2008). Accessible at http://blogs.zdnet.com/feeds/?p=155.

authority issue also emerges when an ecosystem has many separate environments, each with its own set of owners.

Jeremiah Owyang of Forrester Research, a leading analyst firm, described three common approaches to how organizations adopt and implement social systems:[9]

- **Decentralized ("The Tire")**—Adoption occurs anywhere in the organization, with business units or teams working independently. This often occurs when smaller progressive units adopt social computing before the overall organization is formally willing to do so.

- **Centralized or command ("The Tower")**—A central team in the overall organization is responsible for managing all such activities. The organization has agreed to adopt social computing but is looking to establish control over what actually occurs.

- **Center of excellence ("The Hub and Spoke")**—A central team defines best practices and policies, but actual activity occurs across the organization. The organization has agreed that a central team can help guide many independent activities to balance a common experience against individual or team-level goals and styles.

This is also partially inferred in Online Community Research Network's findings[10] (see Figure 6.1): 33% of social environment owners described their community team as part of some existing department (predominantly marketing), 19% identified themselves as having an independent team in the organization, 18% indicated no formal structure, and 17% have community managers throughout the company.

---

[9] Jeremiah Owyang, "Corporate Adoption of Social Media: Tire, Tower, and the Hub and Spoke," on his Web Strategy by Jeremiah blog (18 March 2008). Accessible at www.web-strategist.com/blog/2008/03/18/trends-corporate-adoption-of-social-media-tire-tower-and-the-wheel/.

[10] Online Community Research Network (OCRN), *Online Community Compensation Survey*, Forum One Communications (August 2008). This research report is available to members of the OCRN. You can join the OCRN at http://ocrn.forumone.com.

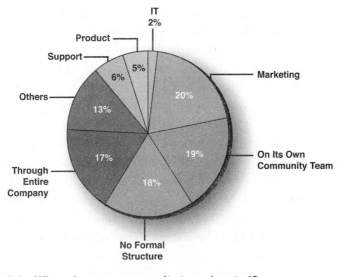

Figure 6.1   Where is your community team located?

(Source: Forum One, Online Community Compensation Survey 2008, *n*=255)

Smaller organizations, or those with fewer groups involved in social systems, can choose to stick to either the decentralized or command models, which can be simpler to manage on smaller scales. However, as an organization moves to deploy social computing more extensively, the eventual direction should be toward a balanced view in a center of excellence model. In this model, a central group (typically led by members from the cross-organizational IT support department) works with members from various teams and departments supporting social environments. This group exists not to command and control all social computing activities, but to act as an information source and coordination point for social computing as it becomes an inevitable part of many functional areas across the organization.

Summary

How multiple social environments or audiences are grouped together into larger entities affects the way the target population can interact. A domain for a social environment defines where potential members are coming from, relative to the organization. Those within the same enterprise might share the same background and culture, but this changes dramatically when the social environment spans boundaries between the organization and specific customers, or exists in the public environment. Having many separate instances of social environments within a larger ecosystem enables the overall population to decide where they want to interact. Alternatively, social environments can also combine multiple tools and social computing methods to enable the same membership to tackle a problem from several angles. Finally, organizations with ecosystems or multiple separate social computing efforts will eventually need to consider how aligned or separate these efforts will be, choosing a decentralized, centralized, or center of excellence approach. These factors of domain and administration help shape the environment's governance policies and the culture to the constituent members.

7

Building a Social Culture

Over time, every organization develops its own culture—whether well defined or unspoken, fragmented or united—simply by virtue of a population sharing in an overall effort. Organizational culture is a combination of the values that the members and employees hold dear, the acceptable behaviors of working with others, the commonly understood language and ideas, and the social norms and standards.

However, sponsoring organizations can choose whether they should directly project their organizational culture into their social environments, strategically choose a different cultural approach, or enable these cultures to develop independently or variably from their sponsor. For example, Disney's Club Penguin, a social environment for children, shares the family-oriented entertainment themes of The Walt Disney Company,[1] which support the desired goals of Club Penguin. Other social experiences might be entirely different from that of the parent organization. Sony Online Entertainment's *Everquest* game, set in a fantasy world of magic and monsters, seems quite dissimilar from the high-end fashion-oriented technology products and appliances that made Sony famous, yet it is contributing as a revenue-generating business product.

Culture can be of strategic value to an organization. Organizational strategies and business processes can deliver poor results or fail when the values and behavior of the group are not aligned with those

---

[1] Club Penguin was a successful independent social experience for children ages 6–14 that The Walt Disney Company acquired in 2007. The similar culture and audience segment of Club Penguin probably helped. Disney also has other social environments and MMOGs: Toontown Online, Pirates of the Caribbean Online, and Disneyfairies.com

strategies. Leaders of the social experience can apply the organizational culture to the experience, depending on how the existing parent culture might support the needs of the social environment's membership. From a social environment's view, culture is also an indicator of how well it is doing and how it is maturing.

As a supporting factor to social strategies and to the health of these systems, identifying, explaining, and promoting culture is an integral aspect of social environments. You need to be able to distinguish elements that define and contribute to culture, and consider these cultural elements in the context of online social experiences.

Defining a Culture for a Social Environment

As described earlier, culture is a combination of the shared values (ideology), acceptable behavior and social norms, and commonly used language and visual imagery. In addition, a group that shares a common culture might collectively remember this information and their history in shared stories and anecdotes. A quick mnemonic of these elements of culture brings together the four key areas: ideology, behavior, imagery, and storytelling (*IBIS*). According to MIT professor emeritus Edgar Schein, one of the founding thinkers of organizational culture, these cultural elements appear in three levels[2] of visibility:

- The *artifact*, or surface level, of identifying objects, structures, and terms that are easy to observe but not necessarily easy to decipher (typically, imagery and stories)
- The espoused *beliefs*, or professed level of official mission statements, strategies, processes, and values that can offer details about what the culture should be (such as espoused ideology, values, and written acceptable behavior)
- The *underlying assumptions* with unspoken, unwritten rules and concepts that the members reinforce over time and eventually internalize (such as unwritten ideology or acceptable behavior)

---

[2] Edgar Schein, *Organizational Culture and Leadership*, 3rd ed. (San Francisco: Jossey-Bass, 2004).

You can tell how ingrained members are in the culture of a social group when they can identify cultural elements on different levels. New members to a social group can discover common stories at the artifact level and read the espoused beliefs, but they need to spend some time and effort absorbing the underlying assumptions in a group.

These levels and elements exist in any type of group, whether members are online or physically in the same location. Social computing culture differs in who defines this culture (leadership model), how they experience it (social experience), who can experience it (domains), and what they can do (tasks) through the capabilities of the online and software-assisted medium.

Ideology and Values

Many social sites identify the topic area or activities that they participate in, but others don't formally define their values and *ideology*.[3] Often the view is that these values will emerge by themselves over time. In other cases, leaders and sponsors implicitly project their own values and attitudes without expressly communicating them to others.

With individual-oriented social experiences, these attitudes and values tend to closely reflect the personality of the owner of the experience. With group-oriented experience models, the leadership model helps identify who defines these values.

When a culture clearly outlines and shares its professed values, prospective members have a basis to consider whether they want to be part of the group. When the values are unspoken, prospective members might need to spend more time investigating the group to make their decision to stay. The time you must spend just trying to understand the group culture is a particularly significant consideration for public-facing environments in which users have many alternatives. Although it might not be possible or desirable to convert

---

[3] In his book *Organizational Culture and Leadership* (San Francisco: Jossey-Bass, 2004), Schein describes **ideology** as either the total set of basic assumptions of the culture or the collection of rationalization for unexplained or superstitious behavior. I use the former definition.

values from the unspoken level to the professed level, it is useful to define and promote professed beliefs.

Some members might be outwardly willing to accept professed values and attitudes, but then express their own hidden values to replace or work around them. Understanding a social group involves investigating the unspoken level of values and attitudes through the lens of the framework of attitudes described earlier. Comparing it to the professed values can give you a clearer picture of the group's ideology.

Behavior and Rituals

Acceptable behavior and rituals come into play when people begin to understand and accept the basic values and ideology of the group. With online experiences, familiarity with the interface and knowledge of how to use the social tool also apply. These behaviors can dictate how to go beyond the functional and use the tools and features in a socially acceptable way.

For example, many e-mail users are familiar with the idea that posting text in ALL CAPITALIZED LETTERS INDICATES THAT THE PERSON IS SHOUTING and that this is frowned upon. This particular etiquette behavior has evolved with e-mail culture, and Internet and social ecosystems have adopted it until it has become almost universal behavior. Other behaviors are specific to the capabilities of each tool. Some social tool developers have turned particular social behaviors into moderated actions integrated into their tool. For example, some social tools enable you to connect to a friend of a friend without asking permission of the initial contact (your friend). However, LinkedIn requires users to direct that request to the friend first and optionally include a message indicating why they want to connect to the friend's friend. These social tools formalize acceptable social behavior in their models, reducing the effort needed to educate members or to police such behavior. In the previous two examples, the acceptable behaviors relate to actions that cause a conflict between a member's preferences and the group's preferences because of a lack of definition.

This intrusion between different cultures, typically between a professional setting and a personal one, can be quite jarring. Dan

Ariely, Duke University professor and author of *Predictably Irrational*,[4] provides an amusing example. Although you must normally pay for your meals in a restaurant, it's commonly considered an insult to pay your parents or your siblings when they invite you to a Thanksgiving or holiday dinner—even when it's appropriate to bring a gift that costs you money. What is acceptable in one cultural environment can easily be unacceptable in another.

If each social environment or ecosystem can have its own sense of acceptable behaviors, how do people learn them? This goes back to the professed and unspoken elements of culture. The holiday dinner example might not break any written rules, placing it on the unspoken level. The user might find out only when someone politely points it out or chides him or her on it. This type of negative reinforcement can work for underlying assumptions if users don't get overzealous in such actions. Positive and negative reinforcement (official or unofficial) can also work in mentoring new users.

The overt means of describing acceptable behavior includes user guidelines, new-user guides, and best practices, expounding on both positive and negative behaviors. This kind of documentation is essential as a population grows larger and the distance between members makes it harder to learn through relationships.

Online environments sometimes provide a *sandbox*, or special designated areas for *newbies*—people new to the environment—to experiment with tools and essentially limit any consequences of improper behavior. This also limits new users' exposure to the potential ire of other members.

Some acceptable behaviors that occur frequently can eventually turn into a ritual for the members. *Rituals* are activities performed on a regular or special-event basis as part of the social experience. A ritual can be as simple as how frequently bloggers post their individual experience, or can involve complex activities such as annual (virtual or real-world) gatherings for community experiences with many activities and sessions for members.

---

[4] Dan Ariely, *Predictably Irrational: The Hidden Forces That Shape Our Decisions* (New York: HarperCollins, 2008).

Individual rituals depend on the social instance and tool. The most common rituals focus on returning to or reconnecting with the social instance to see what is new or to check on relationship interactions. When a user sets up a regular time to perform this task—whether the same time every week, after lunch, or in the evening—that user creates a personal ritual. Responding to comments is just as important as posting one's own thoughts. Such rituals are some of the most basic, but they're important ones to encourage among users because they can increase a user's commitment level beyond the cursory and can help build closer relationships.

Group rituals might require some degree of planning and preparation by a leader. Members might spend just as much time planning and preparing for a group activity—a ritual of its own—because this takes a group to conduct it. In essence, these rituals are best practices on how to conduct a task. The leader needs to know when to apply these practices, what the resource and people requirements are, and how to act on them.

Imagery

Imagery is a summary of the visual and aural concepts associated with a group, such as logos, badges, icons, signals, lingo or jargon, a sound bite or ringtone, or even custom clothing or fashion. Other elements of imagery can be more action oriented, either physically or virtually (such as gestures, handshakes, dances, and so on).

Imagery helps build a social group's story or cultural background. It acts as a clue for other members or nonmembers of the shared persona and ideology of the group. Imagery also serves as an opening for others to inquire about the group—a potential recruiting angle.

Humans tend to be visually oriented, and frequent encounters with the same imagery enable people to recognize them quickly, even in partial form. Marketing groups have exploited this as an element of branding products and ideas. Similarly, social sites and groups can use imagery as a tool to help members identify with the group or with each other:

- **Logos**—Shared visual images are directly associated with the social group.

- **Wearable or expressive virtual goods**—Virtual goods dress a user's profile or space. They can range from virtual analogs to real-world items (such as clothes, furniture, cars, art, posters, and so on), to information mashups and interactive page elements.

- **Social gestures**—Virtual gifts between members associated with emotional value or sympathies can range from common to rare items. Many parallel those in the physical world (such as cards, flowers, or decorations), but others are possible only in the virtual world (such as gravity-defying boots in an online basketball game).

- **Merit badges**—Awards of distinction can be bestowed upon members of the social group when they have achieved or completed some task or test.

Another cultural artifact that builds the imagery and symbolism of a social system is the language and expressions members use. New words can arise when members try to describe their environment, situation, feelings, topic, or activities, as relevant to that social group. As with other cultural elements, leaders and influencers might import words and expressions from other cultures and social groups. Language and expressions unique and original to a particular social environment are better indicators of the growth of the local culture.

On the surface, a group's special lingo helps members communicate with each other faster. Words in this lingo could be verbs, nouns, or adjectives that concisely describe a more complex concept relevant to the group—for example, *poking* or getting poked in Facebook is a quick indication from another member that he or she is noticing you, although the varieties of poking itself have grown into a full range of emotions. Some lingo or imagery has expanded so widely from the original social group that it has become common jargon elsewhere; consider the example of *emoticons*, or smiley faces, which started as a quick communication of feelings via e-mail when the world was all text. Today people can almost universally recognize such emoticons, an outcome of the rise of e-mail.

Below the surface, language helps define bounding relationships: If you don't understand what it means, you aren't really in the group. It's a demarcation point and a reinforcing factor of being in tune with the group. This kind of verbal imagery becomes more important in online groups because direct visual cues or expression through body language doesn't occur. Even though photos and videos have become common in social systems, members who meet in real life still feel apprehension; however, this can dissipate faster when they speak the same language. Imagery can itself be the basis for stories of their origin and value. Knowing the story behind the imagery describes a deeper initiation into the culture.

Storytelling

Stories offer a way to bring together all the other cultural elements and artifacts—converting mundane ideas into memorable experiences for readers and listeners, embedding common vision and social knowledge, teaching skills, or describing strategy.[5] A well-crafted story embeds particular cultural artifacts, such as acceptable behaviors, defined values, or imagery, into the overall narrative. While listeners are building emotional attachments to the characters, artifacts, and ideas in the story, they're learning these cultural elements placed in context.

Stories also represent an alternative means of describing the value of social experiences to others. A social environment might be too complex to understand easily, but sharing a story about how it helps people conveys the value of having such an experience to business managers, sponsors, and prospective members. They can help members with different origins, objectives, and societal cultures come together to normalize themselves to a common social experience. Thus, the greater the diversity of members in a social experience is, the more storytelling is needed as a relationship-binding factor.

Stephen Denning suggests in *The Leader's Guide to Storytelling* that we should use storytelling to create narratives around business objectives, such as sparking action, transmitting values, fostering collaboration, taming rumors, and creating and reinforcing brands.[6]

---

[5] Walter Swap, Dorothy Leonard, Mimi Shields, and Lisa C. Abrams, "Using Mentoring and Storytelling to Transfer Knowledge in the Workplace," *Journal of Management Information Systems* 18, no. 1 (Summer 2001): 95–114.

[6] Stephen Denning, *The Leader's Guide to Storytelling* (San Francisco: Jossey-Bass/John Wiley & Sons, 2005). This is an excellent resource to help business leaders convey ideas, values, and imperatives to their organization in effective ways through creating stories.

Stories help listeners develop an attachment to the more colorful world described in the story compared to the black-and-white volumes of data- and process-oriented business details. In *Personality Not Included*,[7] Rohit Bhargava highlights the significance of making sure that a story shares the following properties:

- **Is it unique?**—Does the story have some aspect that people might not have encountered or thought of before?
- **Is it talkable?**—Does it provide some basis for people to discuss the story?

Both *Personality Not Included* and *Buzzmarketing*[8] suggest story narratives that have worked well in social media.

Culture and Maturity of Social Environments

Cultural artifacts and overt and unspoken values become pervasive across a group over time and with maturity. A social group that develops a complex cultural identity indicates a more mature group in which members have had greater interaction in different situations to create a shared identity and purpose. Conversely, the lack of cultural elements can point to a lack of appreciation or involvement in the social group. This is a significant factor of commitment to a social group—accepting the vision and aligning with the values of the group. Therefore, culture becomes a key part of evaluating the health and progression of a social group through identifying members' commitment. (See Chapter 8, "Engaging and Encouraging Members.")

The social architecture elements of social experience model, leadership model, social task, and domain can shape culture directly or implicitly. By choosing these elements, you might be choosing or encouraging a particular set of values or behavior.

---

[7] Rohit Bhargava, *Personality Not Included* (New York: McGraw-Hill, 2008).
[8] Mark Hughes, *Buzzmarketing: Getting People to Talk About Your Stuff* (New York: Portfolio Trade Books, 2008).

The Cultural Impact of Social Architecture

As indicated at the beginning of this chapter, the culture of a social environment doesn't need to be the same as that of the sponsoring organizations; good reasons often exist to set them apart to fit different strategic directions. However, social architecture elements can predispose a social environment to a particular set of cultural elements, or require leaders and sponsors to choose among several default options. Knowing these predispositions enables you to find a better fit between a specific social architectural model and a strategic need. The four key elements to consider are the social experience, the leadership model, the social task, and the domain.

How Social Experience Models Impact Culture

Social experience models require different approaches to creating cultures, depending on the amount of definition needed and the types of cultural artifacts that are relevant. Table 7.1 shows how the different components of the IBIS can impact each social experience model. These are some suggestions of different types of artifacts within each of the components that leaders can look for and collect, potentially serving as reference items for cultural metrics (for example, how many people in the group recognize the official logo or conduct certain types of rituals).

TABLE 7.1   The IBIS Model in Relation to Each Social Experience Model

	Ideology	Behavior and Rituals	Imagery	Storytelling
Individual	Informally describes the values of individuals and their worldview.	How frequently members post and communicate are rituals. The individual has unique or special rituals to stand out. Acceptable behavior is typically ad hoc.	This includes photos of individuals, their topic, and their activities, as well as merit badges, memberships, and awards.	A strong storytelling possibility exists, with the individual as the protagonist.

TABLE 7.1   The IBIS Model in Relation to Each Social Experience Model

	Ideology	Behavior and Rituals	Imagery	Storytelling
Social network	Informally describes interests and identifies values to members of network.	Acceptable behavior is ad hoc and relative to each member in the social network. Members communicate regularly or occasionally.	This includes photos of individuals, their topic, and their activities, as well as merit badges, memberships, and awards.	A storytelling possibility exists, with the individual as the protagonist. Stories of special events and activities are shared with specific members.
Closed group	Focuses on goals and identifies basic values or approaches to goals.	Members agree on a basic communication process or a course of actions. Acceptable behavior can be planned or ad hoc. Regular meetings or interaction times are scheduled, if only for status updates.	Visual imagery is more relevant the larger and more formal the group becomes.	Updates from members are shared, focusing on ideas that might be useful to other members. The origin story and purpose are maintained in short form.
Visible group	Same as above, but some groups might choose or exhibit different ideology inside the group versus what is visible outside the group.	Same as above, but some groups might choose or exhibit different behavior inside versus behavior visible outside the group.	Same as above, but some groups might choose or exhibit different imagery inside the group versus what is visible outside the group.	Same as above, but some groups might choose or exhibit different stories inside the group versus what is visible outside the group.

TABLE 7.1 The IBIS Model in Relation to Each Social Experience Model

	Ideology	Behavior and Rituals	Imagery	Storytelling
Community	Some espoused values can help focus the incoming members.	Guidelines and policies are helpful and necessary in defining acceptable behavior. Regular open meetings might not be possible for everyone to join but are still useful in building commitment. Leaders engage in regular periodic communication on status with members.	Logos, award, or merit badge systems are awarded, and descriptions of their significance exist. Photos and profiles of leaders and exemplary members are shared.	Lots of possibilities for storytelling exist: origins, activities, meetings, events, awards, new members, successes, and exemplary members.
Mass collaboration	Some espoused values can help focus the incoming members.	Guidelines and instructions on how to collaborate and use available tools are necessary. Acceptable behavior can be formalized or structured through the tools.	Logos or icons are identified to share beyond the collaboration.	Success stories or highlights focus on recent shared activities or wins.

Table 7.1 excludes personal experience for the simple reason that very little culture is unique to this perspective other than what the organization provides. The individual experience informally builds the culture around the ideas, habits, and stories of the owner of the experience. In personal social networks, the ideology and stories still center on the owner, but they need to consider what each connection in their network considers appropriate. In closed and visible groups, the core members develop the cultural elements through their actions over time. The core leadership of a community often

originates the culture. However, because these leaders might be any member of the community, the actual individuals, values, behaviors, and stories can change over time. Mass collaborations typically formalize the acceptable behaviors into a fixed set of controls or functions, but other elements can vary quite significantly in theme and content, depending on the sway of the membership.

How Social Leadership Models Impact Culture

The leadership model for a social experience has an impact on how leaders can influence the culture of a group and how cultural artifacts are crafted, disseminated, or reinforced (see Table 7.2). The key role of leaders is to exemplify the values of the group. In centralized and delegated models that lean toward control over the experience, leaders can set the values and ideology from which other cultural elements begin.

Even if leaders and influencers have a strong say in creating cultural values and artifacts, this doesn't necessarily imply that members will accept or adopt them. Members still have a choice to contradict or ignore the culture. Interestingly, the extremes of alignment toward or against the culture attract the most interest. For example, a public discussion forum on gun ownership will draw members who are enthusiastic advocates and those who are severe opponents. This behavior applies across all leadership models; however, who has impact on the direction of the culture varies.

As we move toward the open leadership or market-oriented leadership models in Table 7.2, the capability to create and distribute the culture spreads out to more members; with a wider spread of this control, it becomes increasingly difficult for any one person to direct or change cultural opinion without the cooperation of others. Leaders have a strong impact in reinforcing artifacts of their choosing, which can lead to greater acceptance by the membership. Cultural weakness enters through poorly articulated or defined values and a lack of artifacts—the responsibility of the leaders.

TABLE 7.2 Impact of Leadership Models on Creating Culture

	Defining Culture	Aligning Members to Culture	Spreading Culture
Centralized	Leaders determine direction and thus have the power to express culture. Leaders might take suggestions from members.	Because members have little say in direction, growth depends on their affinity for and acceptance of the leader's culture.	Leaders are primarily responsible for distributing and reinforcing culture.
Delegated	Delegate leaders determine the direction and thus have the power to express culture. Leaders might take suggestions from members.	Because members have little say in direction, growth depends on their affinity for and acceptance of the leader's culture, although they might have more choice in the delegate leaders.	Delegate leaders are primarily responsible for distributing and reinforcing culture in their areas or across the group.
Representative	The leadership identifies or adopts the culture based on input from the members.	Strong cultures depend on agreement with and adherence to the values and cultural identification that the members define and the leaders gather.	Leaders and members equally share in spreading culture, although leaders might need to reinforce and qualify it.
Starfish	Each subgroup of members can build a local culture while keeping to the core principles and shared values across the experience.	Members accept the overall cultural principles but are free to adapt a local culture, balancing autonomy with shared focus.	Members reinforce and qualify culture among each other.
Swarm	Creators of the experience lay the groundwork for culture, often based on the features of the social tool.	Overall culture needs to be simple to address a mass audience because members decide for themselves.	Culture spreads as part of participation in the experience, or from members drawing others in.

How Social Tasks Impact Cultural Values

All jobs characterize a set of values. The more people commit to the activity, the more those values become part of them. Rescue divers and firemen often face different scenarios each time they go out, requiring them to apply different procedures based on their pragmatic analysis of the situation. Other jobs, such as working as an upholsterer for a line of automobiles, require high levels of consistency. Working on industry standards requires some degree of cooperative values, even though competing companies are involved.

Similarly, each task in an online social environment can impart values to the participants and, therefore, frame a set of shared cultural values even before the participants begin to interact. Members might learn these values as they participate more frequently and encounter situations that convey or reinforce such values.

Some tasks enable multiple possibilities, leaving it to the members or leaders to choose their set of values. For example, the sponsors might want the social group to focus on short-term achievable goals as part of a social brainstorming task, but other situations call for long-term objectives.

The choices might also be in the hands of the members themselves. For example, some people participating in social brainstorming might want to reach people based on pure, rational logic, whereas others choose to inspire people to choose their ideas. Users might even contradict the default value in that dimension. For example, social brainstorming generally pits people's ideas against those of others, but that does not exclude the possibility that people might want to collaborate on a particular idea.

Summary

Culture, an integral part of social environments, can exist in obvious or professed levels, or can hide in the unspoken but shared behavior of members. It emerges as a confluence of shared ideology and values, behavior and rituals, imagery, and stories about the social group. As a concept, culture can be developed, but it first requires understanding what actually exists. In particular, identifying some of the attitudes and values of the group can help prospective members learn about the cultural identity. Understanding the similarities or differences between the culture of a social instance and that of its sponsoring organization also helps prospective members consider whether the culture suits them.

Where members come from, the form of leadership, the social experience model, and the types of social tasks they impact can predispose the membership to particular cultural values or needs. Cultural factors also contribute to both measurement and strategy. Next, we need to look at how culture contributes to engaging members and becomes a way to measure commitment to a social experience.

8

Engaging and Encouraging Members

Accepting and adopting the culture of a social environment depends heavily on a sense of belonging to the environment. This belonging is visible when you see members participate in activities in a social environment by sharing, debating, or rating ideas. However, this type of participation is typically an artifact at the visible surface level of culture. It does not identify the deeper sentiments of belonging to the social group. Understanding the overall sense of belonging requires examining whether members can understand the vision and whether they align themselves with the values of the group.

How members feel and demonstrate belonging gives an indication of their commitment to the social environment. With the software support of online social environments, it is possible to map members' engagement activity. Other tools, such as surveys and polls, can help determine the other senses of belonging. Together this helps identify levels of commitment across different groups of members in an environment. Understanding this distribution can help you see how the population is maturing together as a social group, which is a success factor for getting results from social tasks.

Belonging and Commitment

Social environments depend on the involvement of members in the activities or social tasks set before them. However, the degree of involvement might depend on their sense of belonging and commitment to the purpose of the social group. Some social tasks might require high degrees of commitment before you can reach the right state of mind across the social group to conduct the tasks (see Figure 8.1). In other situations, understanding the degree of commitment is key to the business purpose of the social group, such as a social environment to draw new customers to a product or recruit customer evangelists. Therefore, we need to find ways of identifying the commitment and the sense of belonging to the purpose of a social group.

Etienne Wenger, a leading researcher on community environments, describes three modes of belonging:[1] *imagination, alignment,* and *engagement*. The first mode indicates whether members can see the vision of what is possible or significant ("I see what you see"). The second indicates whether members consider their own values to be in line with the culture and goals of the social environment ("I agree, this is the way to go about it"). The third describes whether members engage in the activities of the social group ("I'm helping to deliver it"). Consider an example from real-world societies: When picking a candidate in an election, voters must consider whether they agree with a candidate's vision on what issues are important, and then whether they agree that the candidate's goals and approach fit their view. If they feel strongly enough, they might even engage in activities with or on behalf of that candidate.

You can have different degrees of belonging in each mode. People might be able to imagine a concept or philosophy (for example, the idea of green energy such as solar power), but they might not necessarily agree with it (alignment) or want to participate in it (engagement). They can also align themselves with the idea (for example, become proponents of alternative energy) or engage in it (such as using solar power for their homes) without seeing a complete vision. They can also engage in it without aligning or sharing in its vision (subscribing to an electric company that generates green power).

Supporting imagination involves defining and communicating a vision to a future goal or situation, and creating a strategy that involves the members to reach them. You need to articulate the value to each member and to the group as a whole. One approach is to

---

[1] Etienne Wenger, *Communities of Practice: Learning, Meaning, and Identity* (Boston: Cambridge University Press, 1998).

outline an example scenario of how members can work or live in the future social environment according to the vision.

A successful vision for a social environment alludes to goals that speak to what the potential members want. Members are stakeholders in the social environment, and the vision needs to meet the needs of these stakeholders, providing value that benefits them directly. Imagination also includes the values that drive the members toward that goal. Chapter 7, "Building a Social Culture," describes how these values shape the alignment of members to the cause.

Of the three modes of belonging, the most visible is how members engage in activity. In social computing, engagement activity is usually easily visible as content or interpersonal actions that the system can log automatically.

Be careful not to base the measure of belonging to a community on engagement and activity alone. As described earlier in the different modes of belonging, members can participate in activity, but this is not a complete picture of their commitment to the system. The activity (engagement) needs to be balanced with the measures of identification with the vision (imagination) and alignment to the values. You can find data for these other metrics through surveys (see Chapter 10, "Measuring Social Environments").

Creating a Model for Identifying Commitment

Because of the many possible ways to build a social environment, we use a general framework to describe commitment as distinct levels. You might need to customize this framework to the specific situation of your social system and the types of data that your social software system is able to collect across all members. One approach is to simply enable members to report their own level of commitment. Unfortunately, basing commitment on members' self-reporting has the inherent bias of primarily identifying only the vocal minority and typically those seeking attention. Self-reporting can be useful but needs to be balanced with other ways of identifying commitment. A second question is whether their espoused commitment can be validated in some manner, perhaps through completing particular types of tasks that can be considered achievements.

If your social environment supports identities and can attribute individual actions to each identity, then you might have an advantage in gathering commitment metrics. However, gathering information that can identify individuals personally is a controversial action that can be unpopular or even considered illegal in some countries.

Looking at aggregate metrics across the entire population requires identifying trends instead of examining each person's history. However, you can still fit this aggregate behavioral information into the context of a given framework by separating commitment into distinct threshold levels and watching for markers of certain types of actions that fit profiles of behavior for each level.

In Figure 8.1, the mountain is a representation of the different levels of commitment across the entire social group. Each layer designates a particular profile of measurable behavior that identifies the level of commitment across the group. This model[2] is based on Abraham Maslow's theory of humanistic psychology, which has influenced many fields of understanding human behavior. Maslow's Hierarchy of Needs[3] describes how humans are willing to behave on different levels when they feel secure enough at a lower level. Maslow's model begins with basic physiological needs such as breathing, food, water, and warmth. Secure in this, people are more willing to concentrate on the next level of needs—physical safety. Then they progressively move up the hierarchy, depending on security and confidence at each level: the need for love, affection, and belongingness; the need for esteem; and the need for self-actualization leading them to issues of morality, spirituality, and ideas of a higher purpose for themselves.

With online social environments, we can probably assume that a person has been fed and is physically safe before that person starts

---

[2] This approach is also based on an idea shared by Art Gould, a former community manager at AMD Corp., from his talk at the 2007 Evans Data Developer Relations Conference. The idea of applying Maslow's model is not unique; a number of other social computing thought leaders have expressed this view.

[3] Abraham H. Maslow, *Toward a Psychology of Being*, 3rd ed. (New York: John Wiley & Sons, 1999).

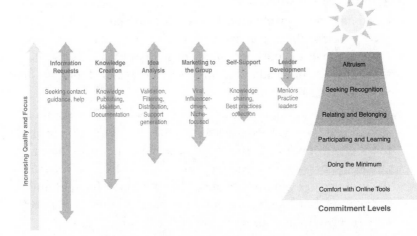

Figure 8.1   A generic framework for identifying commitment

socializing over a network with others. Therefore, the levels in this model focus on different levels of needs for security:

- **Comfort with online tools**—Not everyone is equally comfortable working and interacting with others online. This might sound strange to users who grew up using such tools, but many users still barely interact with others online. This is the bare-minimum level users must overcome to develop commitment to a social environment.

- **Doing the minimum**—These users visit the site to consume information that they might find, but they have not developed any attachment to it as a resource or to any members within.

- **Participating and learning**—These members are familiar with the environment or are comfortable enough to return more often. They start interacting with other members, asking questions, and posting thoughts. Many spend time trying to better understand the culture, learn or identify the leaders, and question the goals.

- **Relating and belonging**—These members have already developed relationships with more than a few members, and they interact on a regular (by their definition) basis with the group. They understand the basics of the culture, know some of the leaders, and might participate in some activities, but are not yet comfortable or well known enough to become leaders.

- **Seeking recognition**—Some members might be interested in becoming more involved in the social experience and seek to receive recognition as a leader in some role. These tend to be some of the most active members, contributing frequently, participating in or leading group activities, and building or strengthening relationships.

- **Altruism**—The final level are members whom the membership already recognizes as leaders, either because of their history of contributions to the social instance or because they are already well known as leaders in the topic elsewhere (beyond the instance or even the domain). They have excellent potential as mentors, but they might not participate with every request they receive because they are in high demand.

The markers of behavior for these commitment levels depend on the design of the social environment, but Table 8.1 illustrates some common examples of how they identify belonging.

TABLE 8.1 Markers of Commitment Levels

Commitment Level	Engagement	Imagination	Alignment
Comfort with online tools	Displays little or no use of social tools (discover through survey)	Doesn't agree with or recognize the vision or purpose of the social tool	Exhibits little or no identification with the values
Doing the minimum	Has basic familiarity with the social environment, but only one-time or initial visits (discover through survey)	Exhibits low identification with the vision	Exhibits little or no identification with the values
Participating and learning	Forms relationships, discovers or rates content	Exhibits medium identification with the vision	Exhibits medium identification with the values; doesn't communicate disagreements on values

TABLE 8.1   Markers of Commitment Levels

Commitment Level	Engagement	Imagination	Alignment
Relating and belonging	Signs up for activities; has some initial forays into commenting on others' content; distributes content	Exhibits high identification with the vision	Exhibits high identification with the values; might seek guidance on values the user does not agree with
Seeking recognition	Is active in many content and interpersonal actions; contributes some highly rated content; initiates or leads activities; actively seeks others in need and responds	Exhibits high identification with the vision; contributes to the evolution of the vision	Exhibits high identification with values or openly shares disagreements on values; communicates values to others; applies or promotes espoused culture and artifacts
Altruism	Leads activities and mentors others; attracts people looking for help; frequently is referenced or cited in conversation; contributes highly rated or accessed content.	Exhibits high identification with the vision; leads or defines the vision, or contributes to its evolution	Exhibits high identification with values or openly shares disagreements on values; communicates values to others; applies or promotes espoused culture and artifacts

Although the "mountain" pictured in Figure 8.1 might allude to a need to progressively climb through the commitment levels, this is not necessary for all members. You should count on a population distribution conceptually similar to the size implied by the layers in the image.

Figure 8.1 also shows different ranges (on the left side of the figure) that describe general levels for commitment that can factor into supporting the types of social tasks. For example, requests for information or help are some of the easiest to obtain in many social environments if members can imagine that they might get some response—often just the proximity of others in the same role or experts who could address the problem is enough to encourage doing the minimum. This does not necessarily mean that their requests will get answered, but the possibility of getting help through this channel still exists.

For a social group such as a community to become self-support-ing and answer most of its own questions, relatively higher degrees of commitment among some of its members are needed—in particular, members with a strong sense of belonging and those offering their help to gain recognition in the community. The group needs people who willingly pay attention to requests for help and are self-motivated to spend the time to consider the problem and provide their views.

When members start to appear at these higher levels of commit-ment, it also indicates the growing maturity of the membership of the social environment.

Maturing over a Lifecycle

Commitment levels provide a way to look at the membership forming and evolving as a social group over a lifecycle, going through a number of stages from conception to dissolution. Taking this strategic view of the growth or maturity makes it easier to plan for operations and identify what members need. In an ecosystem or col-lection of many similar social environments, understanding maturity can help the leaders develop a way to monitor and compare the health of the different social groups across these collections.

Many community and social strategists have frequently men-tioned that any social group takes time to eventually mature to a point at which it becomes self-sustaining and most productive. The goal of the maturity lifecycle is to describe the right conditions, not time, to reach this productivity. Consider the left side of Figure 8.1, which indicates different behaviors from the social group that depend on having members at the designated commitment levels. The maturity lifecycle in Table 8.2 describes the stages in which committed users at these levels begin to appear. The table also aims to assist leaders in determining their course of actions to further the group to maturity.

Although Table 8.1 provides a way to identify the ratios of mem-bers at different commitment levels in a social group, maturity describes what these ratios should be by breaking down the lifecycle into observable stages (see Table 8.2). The maturity lifecycle also looks beyond just the commitment levels of members, into their cul-ture, actions, and network structure.

Whether all social instances in an ecosystem evolve according to a common pattern is debatable, but this idea of a lifecycle is not unprecedented. The Institute for Knowledge Management (IKM) identified developmental stages of a community of practice, a particular model of a social environment, as a graph of activity over time, although this is purposely imprecise.[4]

Metrics provide ways to look backward (to results) or forward (to determine strategy). Using a lifecycle helps provide guidance as a prediction tool. Prediction is an active hobby for many people, but, at best, it is still an educated guess. This "education" can come through observing other social instances that follow a similar pattern, looking for similarities to determine the lifecycle stages.

The lifecycle stages can help leaders determine the operational activities they need to focus on for a particular social instance. The early stages might call for a greater need to facilitate relationship building and recruit key individuals, whereas the latter stages might emphasize task completion and members mentoring other members. The dissolution stage from Table 8.2 indicates that members are starting to leave in numbers greater than normal turnover. When this occurs, leaders must investigate the reasons behind the dissolution or dispersal of members to determine whether members are merging with or transitioning to another social instance, or whether an abnormal situation is occurring (such as a loss of key influencers and leaders, instability and dissent among members, and so on).

---

[4] Michael A. Fontaine, "Keeping Communities of Practice Afloat: Understanding and Fostering Roles in Communities," *Knowledge Management Review* 4, no. 4 (September/October 2001): 16–21.

TABLE 8.2   A Framework for Mapping the Maturity of Social Environments

	Conception	Initial	Nascent	Active	Mature	Dissolution
Description	Before launch. Sponsors can plan the design or populate the instance with initial content.	Immediately after launch. The instance is available to the population (even if part of a beta program).	Some members keep returning, and relationships are forming.	Members actively interact with each other and join in task participation.	Members actively participate in tasks; the instance has a stable membership.	The instance is reaching a normal end of life, either intentionally or abnormally.
Imagination	Sponsors can define the vision for members.	Users are trying to understand the vision.	Users are weighing the significance of the vision or the value of membership	Most members understand and accept the vision.	Members are evangelizing the vision to others.	Members disagree with the current vision.
Alignment	Leaders can define the initial set of values.	Members are trying to identify the initial values.	Members accept the initial values.	Most members accept the shared values but might evolve them as well.	Shared values have stabilized and are well accepted.	Members seek new values (or vision).
Engagement	No engagement other than planning activities.	Little or no engagement.	Members join into the simplest or most common activities.	Members frequently participate in regular activities, with emerging recognition and altruism actions.	Members participate in long-term activities, and it's easy to identify highly committed members.	Established members and leaders stop coming or participating in activities.

TABLE 8.2 A Framework for Mapping the Maturity of Social Environments

	Conception	Initial	Nascent	Active	Mature	Dissolution
Cultural elements	Initial cultural elements are created (such as logos) before adoption.	Members experience little or no identification with the culture or its artifacts.	A few new cultural artifacts are emerging and being tested.	Cultural artifacts (such as stories and lingo) spread rapidly; unaccepted artifacts die off.	Stabilization and wide acceptance of cultural artifacts takes place.	The culture might not change, but the climate does.
Traffic metrics	Not valid before launch.	The instance has unique visitors but few return visitors, or low registrations.	Membership is growing and the instance has some return visitors.	The site undergoes a high growth in new or return visitors.	Membership growth rate is slowing, but return visitors are relatively high and steady.	Overall traffic is dropping.
Structural metrics	Not valid before launch.	Few or no connections exist yet.	Some initial connections and networks are forming.	Active connections exist among members, and members are starting to accept roles.	Networks are changing minimally; new connections can still form.	Networks are shrinking.

Programs to Grow or Encourage Your Social Group

Instead of observing the commitment and maturity of members, social environment leaders and community managers (see Chapter 9, "Community and Social Experience Management") can try to encourage and progress member involvement. Some people would argue that taking a directed approach to growing a social group interferes with the natural development of the group. This is particularly relevant for ecosystems of social environments in which many instances bloom or wither by their own accord, but the ecosystem as a whole continues. However, when the business depends on every social environment to succeed, this activity can accelerate the maturity toward productivity.

Leaders can take a number of approaches by applying programs to encourage positive behaviors that improve their commitment and involvement. In particular, we're interested in how these programs can leverage the power of working in a social situation: rewarding positive behaviors publicly, encouraging cross-training and mentoring, and involving reputation and roles of the membership.

Membership Reward Programs

Membership reward programs encourage members to maintain their participation in a social instance by rewarding good behavior or their achievements. Although reputation systems in social computing enable members to signify trust and competence of other members, reward programs signify the trust relationship between the member and the leadership of the social environment. They both follow similar structure and processes: Both can have points, weighted points, thresholds, and achievements; and they both require some qualification and awarding processes. However, leaders create reward programs to enable specific behavior for the sponsor's interest, or to guide the long-term maturity of the environment itself (see Table 8.3). Reward programs are a tool to keep people interested and engaged in the environment, either to contribute to other members or to participate in directed activities from the sponsor.

TABLE 8.3   Rewarding Members

	Rewards for Sponsor Goals	Rewards for Social Group Goals	Reputation System
Purpose	Tasks or goals are specified by sponsors.	Commitment and maturity of the social group is encouraged, as is support for the group's activities.	Relationship building, resource identification, and roles are encouraged.
Interaction	Social interaction with others is not required.	Social interaction might be encouraged.	Social interaction is always encouraged.
Individual versus group action	Members can achieve as individuals or as groups of people.	Members can achieve as individuals or as groups of people.	Reputation is based on each individual's work.
Competition	Members can compete for rewards or achieve them independently.	Members can compete for rewards or achieve them independently.	Members compete for reputation.

A reward program must avoid bias and complaints of unfairness. Programs are often based on identifiable actions that can be verified or measured. You do not need to explain how you weigh or value these actions, but you do need to explain what you are looking for so members can work in the directed intentions of the program. Because of social computing's software-assisted medium, you can integrate the capability to track activity in the social environment with the reward system. Creating a reward system for your social group usually requires the following steps:

1. Identify the goals of the reward program for participants. What is in it for the participant? What benefits do they get?

2. Identify the goals of the program for the sponsors. What sponsor initiatives or programs does rewarding members support?

3. Determine the qualification characteristic and process for each metric. Do you want to measure individual activities, the output or achievement from these activities, or their peers' evaluation of their contributions? Do you need to rank participating members?

4. Choose your metric types and units that meet those goals. Are the steps of the program measurable in terms of points, threshold levels, testimonials, unique achievements, or other metrics?

5. Determine the award process for each metric. Does the system automatically award members, or do you need to manually review and award them?

6. Determine the presentation format. What form of award or reward do members actually receive? Is it a physical award or a virtual one that exists only in the social environment? Can they show this to others, and how do they do so?

7. Document the process, metrics, and values. Have you provided documentation to candidate members so that they understand all aspects of the program?

Some behaviors can fit simultaneously into both a reward program and a reputation program. For example, you might want to reward members based on how frequently they contribute to a site, and you might want to publicize this reward to foster these members' reputation as frequent contributors. The former improves the level of trust the sponsoring organization has in the member; the latter improves the level of trust that the social group has in that member. Therefore, such an action contributes to both programs.

Recruiting Evangelists and Advocates

Instead of providing rewards to encourage activity participation, a second approach involves peer-to-peer advocacy and encouragement. In this situation, leaders identify and elect specific members as advocates or evangelists based on some assessment of high commitment levels. In particular, the members should show a relatively high degree of alignment and imagination toward the goals of the social group and demonstrate capability to convince others of the vision and values.

Member advocates and customer evangelists tend to fit a common profile of people who are motivated more by recognition than by gifts. Microsoft's MVP and Oracle, Inc.'s ACE[5] programs focus on recruiting customers as product evangelists in their public-facing communities for developers and product users.[6] Similarly, IBM's Social Software Enablement team uses a program to recruit employees as volunteer ambassadors to reach out to their peers within the enterprise.[7]

Although such programs can provide gift rewards, evangelists typically indicate that recognition is their primary motivator. This recognition can come in several forms:

- *Public acknowledgment in the social group* in one or more forms: imagery, such as awarding merit badges (for example, the Oracle ACE program has a special graphic for such leaders) for the members' specialty or as a marker of their privileged position, publishing announcements and stories about the leaders, or ranking members on a publicized list as a leader board.

- *Special access either to information or to leaders* in the sponsoring organization in ways that others do not have. This can be a continual element such as a special Web site or channels in your social site that are available only to these members. The program can also be event based, such as offering special meet-ups and conferences for just this audience. Social group leaders should also respond to these members quickly and urgently.

- *Swag or gifts* have less of an impact, except when they describe evangelists' special status to others.

---

[5] The Oracle ACE program focuses on candidates nominated by members of the Oracle Technology Network community. Each ACE or ACE Director receives a special badge shown in this online community. See www.oracle.com/technology/community/oracle_ace/index.html.

[6] The Microsoft Most Valued Professional program focuses on voluntary technical community leaders who have demonstrated high-quality expertise in offline and online communities (see http://mvp.support.microsoft.com/).

[7] Gina Poole, "IBM Web 2.0 Goes to Work," *O'Reilly & Associates Web 2.0 Expo Europe*, Berlin (October 2008). Presentation slides are available online at www.slideshare.net/gpoole/ibm-web-2-0-goes-to-work-presentation-671274.

Although these reward methods are useful, you must make sure the methods don't fall into the following traps:

- **Having an inadequate description of qualifying requirements**—Arguments will arise over who qualifies, which can be disastrous. Focus on creating objective measures.

- **Having too low requirements and too many candidates**—The idea is not to have as many of these members as you want, but to work with the top ones. Choose a cutoff that matches how much overhead you or your own organization can handle. Having more evangelists than leaders can support is worse than not having enough evangelists.

- **Constantly marketing to members**—You want to share ideas and messages with members, but they'll start revolting against you if it becomes oppressive.

- **Creating a one-sided view**—A program in which everyone is super-enthusiastic about your organization can prompt the rest of the community to see these leaders as sycophants to the sponsors. Get dissenting opinions involved. You don't have to convert them; just involve them to share your side of the story.

- **Not changing the evangelists over time**—Evangelists can grow in relevance over time, but it is more important to show that you are growing along with the community by involving new candidates and, therefore, diversity of ideas. Be careful to state that the program has a time limit, such as one year or six months.

Member Training and Mentoring Programs

Training and mentoring programs aim to educate members through a structured and an unstructured approach, respectively. These programs are useful when the social instance focuses on building the skill or knowledge levels of members, and both novices and adept members are available.

Building a training program can sound like a complex process to develop the right criteria for evaluating members. However, if a highly structured certification program is not necessary, social computing methods can do the job. The program can focus on engaging the adept members to capture their knowledge (see Chapter 5, "Social Tasks:

Collecting and Managing Information") in short bursts, and perhaps create a stream of such activity. Social group leaders can help by giving some structure (with the expertise of others) to the captured knowledge, grouping similar topics, or placing them in sequence. This bottom-up approach of building larger structures of knowledge from smaller tidbits can reduce the time needed in initially planning the training topics, and make it easier to collect the knowledge.

Mentoring is a better choice when the knowledge is less codified and a person needs to learn through experience. A simple approach to enabling members is to develop a program that helps match interested learners with more experienced members, to shadow their activities. Visual, online, multiplayer games can offer a way for a user to shadow a mentor and learn by watching or listening. However, this can also occur by regularly reading the posts or listening to the podcasts of mentors through Web feeds. The goal is to become an active listener, to create a relationship with the mentor, and to ask questions. Social group leaders can help by organizing the matchmaking process, recruiting mentors, and initiating and checking on these relationships.

Summary

Encouraging members to participate toward the purpose or goals of a social environment requires a closer look into the different modes of belonging or commitment to a group: imagination, alignment, and engagement. Social software can make it easy to examine engagement through the activity log of the social group. However, to get a more accurate picture of commitment, you need to consider surveying members to determine their acceptance of the vision and their alignment with the values to achieve that vision.

Understanding commitment in this manner enables you to build a map of the commitment levels of members to study the overall trends and members' sentiments in a social environment. This framework for understanding commitment also fosters a different view of the social group's health, by examining the growth of a social group in a maturity lifecycle. This lifecycle can help social group leaders consider the actions they need to take to develop the group.

Social leaders can also take a tactical approach to encouraging and developing a group by enacting specific programs, such as member rewards, training, peer involvement, and advocacy. These programs are well suited to those who engage in particular activity roles. These programs take effort and planning that often requires dedicated leadership to oversee the growth of the social group and environment, which is the subject of the next chapter.

9

Community and Social Experience Management

Joi Ito, CEO of Creative Commons and a venture capitalist, compared completing quests in massively multiplayer games such as *World of Warcraft* to conducting a symphony.[1] Rituals involve members taking on certain transitory roles during the event; only when they act in harmony and synchrony can they meet the end goals. This level of group harmony relies on all participants knowing the situation they face and the actions they need to perform. The participants might need guidance about when to perform their part, and perhaps some help in performing it. A guild leader, community manager, or similar role can help in these situations. This leader's job is not to order people around, but to elicit their help and participation in the ritual. By Gary Hamel's definition[2]—management is a way to aggregate the efforts of people—this is the same concept that traditional business management attempts to solve. Leading a social experience might just be a newly evolved form of management.

Whether you call them managers, bureaucrats, politicians, leaders, or heroes, they are all approaches to the job of guiding people to cooperate in a task. Social environments are no different. The job of a *community manager* (CM), the widely used title in social

---

[1] Joi Ito, from his session on the social aspect of massively multiplayer games, at the O'Reilly Web 2.0 Summit, San Francisco (November 2006).

[2] Bill Breen and Gary Hamel, *The Future of Management* (Boston: Harvard Business School Press, 2007).

computing,[3] is an interdisciplinary role unlike the direct management or leadership in other types of work groups. As indirect influencers, CMs are typically shepherds of social environments, guiding or tending to a disparate flock of active minds and motives toward a common purpose.

A CM's job can involve several different roles: developing relationships among members, promoting the activities and goals of the community, and executing administrative and governance duties. In an organization, they can fit into many functions: marketing, product support, IT, public relations, business development, innovation development, project management, human resources, and even sales. These roles point to a multidisciplinary set of responsibilities and tasks, sometimes too much for just a single person or a single set of skills. The business values they provide are primarily in how they enable other business functions, serving as bidirectional channels between the organization and the customers, employees, or partners involved in a social environment.

The Value and Characteristics of a Community Manager

To understand the value of this job role, we need to distinguish between what the CMs offer and what the social environment as a whole provides. We also need to separate their job tasks from the value outcomes they can achieve. Because they function as an intermediary between the sponsoring organization and the membership, we also need to separate the value they bring to the company from what they offer members (see Table 9.1).

---

[3] I'm not particularly a fan of this job title because this role can apply to more social experiences than just the community model. However, this is an industry-adopted term as suggested by the following survey: Forum One Networks, *Online Community ROI: Models and Reports* (San Francisco/Washington, D.C: Current Practice Research, March 2008).

TABLE 9.1   The Value of Community Managers

Direction	Value
To members	Improving relationships with members by providing a human face to an organization or a large social group
	Bringing the value of their own relationships and contact networks within the organization
	Arbitrating conflicts between members, or between the member and the sponsoring organization
	Coordinating member projects and activities
	Serving as a repository of situational knowledge about the organization, the members, or the content
To the sponsoring organization	Serving as an organizational spokesperson to the membership
	Providing a view into the climate of the members about the topic or purpose (the business climate within the enterprise, across business partners, or across the industry)
	Housing a repository of situational knowledge about members, the content, or the topic
	Encouraging and monitoring member involvement and participation in the topics that interest the sponsor
	Resolving issues members might have with the organization
	Measuring and describing value or outcomes of the social group
	Identifying talent and potential for hires or rehires

The value CMs bring to an organization also applies in different ways to the different business functions they serve, which can differ depending on the domain of social users they reach[4] (see Tables 9.2 and 9.3). Although these tables describe how CMs can apply to different social domains, a CM might not be needed for all social experience and government models, especially those that do not rely on leaders directly (see the sidebar "Does Every Social Experience Require a Community Manager?").

---

[4] Connie Benson, "ROI of a Community Manager," Community Strategist blog (28 July 2008). Accessible at http://conniebensen.com/blog/2008/07/27/roi-of-a-community-manager/.

TABLE 9.2   Supporting Customers or Partners

Audience (Domain)	Business Function	Value Added
Customers or business partners (public-facing, cross-boundary, third-party)	Marketing or sales	Increasing the number of touches with customers
		Identifying customer evangelists and activists
		Discovering industry trends and customer interests
		Acting as marketing liaisons to customers
		Guiding marketing on appropriate messaging or tactics
	Product development and delivery	Assisting in gathering product requirements from audience
		Conducting market research with customers
		Identifying competitor activity or offerings
		Conducting design tests and product beta-testing
		Delivering products to customers online
	Customer relations or product support	Providing a human interface to the organization or social group
		Serving as a "finger on the pulse" of audience concerns
		Helping partners locate internal representatives or departments
		Helping customers find appropriate support resources
		Identifying troubled or exiting customers

The multidisciplinary role of CMs involves work in a number of different fields, including marketing and communications, editing and publishing, business process definition, relationship management, training and instructional development, business management and planning, and even a little showmanship. Their wide range of job functions often raise confusion, compared to complementary roles in the areas they serve. The sidebar "What Community Managers Are Not" describes some of these confusing areas.

TABLE 9.3   Supporting Employees and Alumni

Audience (Domain)	Business Function	Value Added
Employees and former employees (enterprise, cross-boundary, third-party)	Resource identification	Facilitating requests to locate specific types of resources
		Helping others create relationships across departments and the organizational structure to identify resources
		Keeping track of innovation projects and employee opportunities
		Identifying best practices and exemplary contributors
		Identifying useful workflows and alternatives to processes
		Managing content and content providers
	Skills and career development	Assisting in finding appropriate mentors and serving as mentors themselves
		Discovering other job or project opportunities internally
		Discovering, promoting, and providing opportunities to top talent
		Evaluating and identifying talent with "soft" people skills
	Organizational changes	Communicating changes to reporting structures and organizational hierarchy
		Maintaining or developing relationships with representatives in a changed environment to continue operations
		Addressing employee issues from changes that occur
	Employee transitions	Attracting, identifying, and recruiting new talent
		Assisting new hires in assimilating to the organizational culture
		Assisting transitional employees who are retiring
		Managing and maintaining relationships with exiting employees
		Identifying potential rehires from a base of former employees

Does Every Social Experience Require a Community Manager?

The many examples and scenarios in this book should illustrate that social experiences come in many shapes and sizes. Do these different experience models obviate the need for a CM?

In some cases, social experiences might not need a full-time person in such a role. However, in many cases, someone might need to take up the mantle of a CM. In the individual experience, owners might take action to market their blog or other social environment instance to others, gather and share the results, and develop relationships with other individuals. A defined group might have no single leader, but the group as a whole still performs the tasks of a CM, especially when undertaking joint projects. A starfish-governed environment simply distributes these responsibilities to volunteers spread across the membership. A mass collaboration might not require as much relationship building among members, but it likely still needs someone to collect results and share them with stakeholders and the members, or prevent abuse of the voting system.

What Community Managers Are Not

Before we can examine what skills, personality traits, and tasks are common to CMs, we need to look at what CMs are not:

- They are usually not people managers assigning and directing tasks to members of the community, even when a team of CMs might exist under a manager.

- They are not an aggregated identity (such as "The Support Team") under which to hide. This makes it difficult for the members to form relationships with them, and can create confusion or distrust in the CM's position on issues.

- They are not developers or programmers who create, build, and administrate the platform infrastructure. Developers can get too many demands for fixes or improvements, which can sometimes hurt their relationships with individual members.

- They are not the primary content creators, such as authors, writers, or editors working to maintain fresh content within group social experiences. They initially might need to contribute content, but this eventually evolves to growing content from the community.

- They are not the subject matter experts. Instead, their job is to engage others in the social experience.

- They are not "willows"—their job is not simply to bend at every whim of a member—nor are they whips to make sure members stay in line. Although CMs are advocates for their social group, they are also representatives for their sponsors and need to have a balanced view.

Mistaking these tasks can harm the social group, the CM's credibility, or the CM's success in carrying out tasks.

Personality Traits and Habits

A CM's responsibilities go beyond the typical member actions on content, people, and the environment. CMs instead focus on tasks that enable these actions and encourage members to participate in them. This requires particular personality traits or job skills that support their tasks:

- **Listening**—A large part of a CM's role is being responsive to the members of the social group, noting their issues and tone, and having the patience and willingness to put things aside to pay careful attention to issues and problems.

- **Talking**—Writing or talking about their experiences, ideas, events, or other insight in a natural or casual tone helps users get to know the CMs better. This is not about marketing or making sales pitches, nor is it an extensive academic or official report.

- **Taking notes**—Good CMs are always taking notes, literally or mentally, and saving or organizing them in a retrievable fashion. In a conversation, they are listening carefully and taking notes on the key points the other person is trying to make. If CMs need to write something down, they can ask users for permission to take notes. With problem issues, CMs might perform the physical act of note taking, either with pen and paper or through tagging and writing online; mental notes often get lost or forgotten. The notes saved are helpful in other activities.

- **Building relationships**—Listening and talking sets a frame to build relationships with members. This is not just remembering the names of members, but also paying careful attention to their motivations, interests, activities, relationships, and other facets of their lives.

- **Engaging in remote or virtual interactions**—Being comfortable working in an environment in which you might never physically meet the users you work with is important. Online environments frequently do not require a physical office location, giving CMs the freedom to work from home or other venues. This also means having the responsibility to actually perform work in such a remote environment and to avoid distractions. However, this is not exclusive; knowing how to interact with members you have never met in face-to-face situations is also useful.

- **Energizing members**—A good CM's personality engages and energizes the people he or she talks to. These CMs like to shine the light on others' activities and bring awareness to such activities they consider significant.

- **Mediating**—Within any social group, some degree of debate or argument eventually will arise. CMs can play a role in mediating or arbitrating when things get rough. They don't need to be the ones to find every solution—it's better if the parties come up with a proposed solution—but they need to be open and seen as neutral.

- **Voicing for the membership**—CMs might need to negotiate with other parties—whether competing for attention in the same organization or working with other sites, events, or groups—to bring attention to their own community or members. CMs should be able to act as a voice for the overall group to the sponsoring organization or to other groups.

- **Finding a way**—CMs must handle a variety of issues—some I see occurring repeatedly, and others are fairly unique. CMs need to have a drive to find a way to solve problems. This means persistence, intelligence, creativity, social awareness, and more. No template exists for this role—it requires an instinctual nature of wanting to help people.

Although the people in a social experience are not employees who directly report to CMs in the way people report to managers in an organization, it is not coincidental that some of these skills are useful to both CMs and people managers. CMs might have a harder job because members do not necessarily have the same commitment and duties as the direct-report employees of people managers. In addition, as more organizations bring social computing into their fold, the skill sets of CMs might eventually parallel those of people managers—or even merge with or transform them entirely. Therefore, it is important to understand the differences in responsibilities and to know what it takes to develop benevolent trust and commitment among members in a social group.

Where Do Community Managers Fit in an Organization?

CMs in the industry often argue against part-time involvement because of the time commitment needed to build relationships and work with many people. This could be particularly relevant to those who run a social environment that involves more than a dozen members, particularly instances of the community experience model. For example, a team collaboration social activity might not require a full-time CM, but a community with hundreds of members will likely require one or more CMs.

As the collaborative behavior in social computing becomes more common and pervasive in organizations, these skills might be relevant to most office and knowledge-worker jobs at some level. Forrester Research consultant Josh Bernoff predicts that, in the future, social computing "will become so common a way to do business that we won't talk about it anymore."[5] Not only will the formal role of a dedicated CM become more prevalent, but some of the CM's skills will

---

[5] John Fortt, "Michael Dell 'Friends' His Customers," Fortune.com (September 2008). Accessible at http://money.cnn.com/2008/09/03/technology/fortt_dell.fortune/.

eventually become a common part of the jobs of technical, manage-rial, and business people in all types of organizations.

For full-time CMs, the Online Community Compensation Survey 2008 offers some insight into how these jobs are structured and com-pensated (see Figure 9.1). Although many organizations have official titles of CM, people who perform this job or lead a team of CMs also carry many titles at other organizations and, commensurate with experience or responsibilities, are paid at different levels.[6] Most are salaried, although some organizations choose to staff their social envi-ronments with part-time entry-level support personnel.

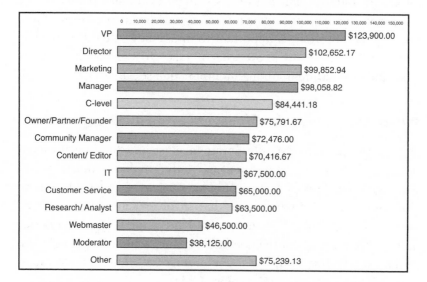

Figure 9.1 Community manager job titles and compensation (*Source: Forum One, Online Community Compensation Survey 2008, n=255*)

The location of CM positions in different parts of the company not only indicates how social systems are helpful to different groups,

---

[6] CMs in a wide variety of industries and organizational types responded to this survey, including online community organizations, media companies, nonprof-its, universities, software companies, government agencies, nongovernmental organizations, and manufacturers. Although 75% were from the United States, the rest came from 19 other countries, from Brazil, to Jordan, to China. This partially explains the differences in titles and pay levels.

but also gives an idea of the different skills necessary to create and maintain a social environment.

Community Manager Tasks and Responsibilities

To provide the business value and achieve some of the objectives described earlier, CMs provide a number of common services:

- Guide and grow the membership and member relationships
- Guide and grow the content and member education and awareness
- Communicate the activity and results of the community
- Assist marketing programs and business development
- Manage the software and social system

Figure 9.2 expands the detail on these many responsibilities often tasked to CMs. Not every situation, social experience, or governance model calls for every one of these responsibilities. However, the tasks that CMs face can vary not just in terms of the structure of the social environment, but also in the CMs' individual style of working with their members.

Member and Relationship Development

A CM's people-focused actions fall mostly into the tasks of building relationships with members and among members. CMs help members become more interactive with the social instance and with each other. This kind of assistance can involve several areas: social tools training, member participation, leader development, personal social development, and member issue management.

Becoming active in a social computing environment first requires getting comfortable with using the software tools. Even users who are familiar with other social tools might not yet be familiar with the tool in a particular instance. Getting started might be fairly straightforward to some experienced users, but most others might need the help of a documented guide or tips on using these tools. This CM task involves creating training content about the tools and either providing the training

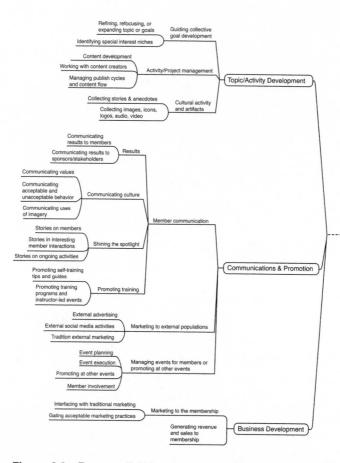

Figure 9.2   Responsibilities of a community manager

in a self-assist manner or, better yet, providing short training sessions on the tools. Using the guided approach tends to work better than assuming that users will read the self-guided information. Another option is to create a simple program for existing members to guide new members.

Chapter 8, "Engaging and Encouraging Members," described how to develop member participation by recruiting new members directly from other populations. Beyond promoting the social instance to other mass audiences, the goal is to find specific individuals that the CM considers directly significant to the social instance, typically as a subject matter expert or a knowledgeable person in that particular field. This can be a casual or temporary role, but the goal is to draw conversations through experts. This includes introducing members to

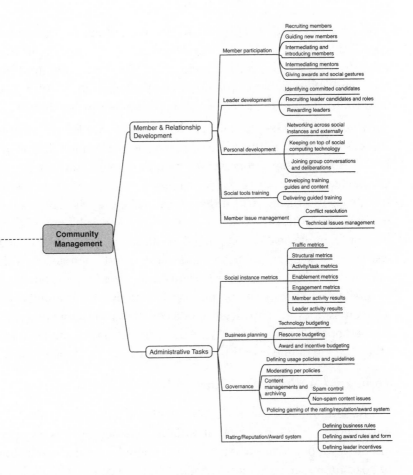

other members they might find relevant, often in relation to some topic in discussion or some activity that is underway. New members might also need encouragement from mentors who have gone through similar experiences. Finally, a CM might introduce member participation awards or offer a system for members to exchange social gestures, to entice members to become more involved.

Whoever the members are, a CM should always be prepared to handle issues from members, whether it is a problem they have with some content or tool function of the social instance, or whether the problem is with other members. Even if no immediate solution exists, CMs must acknowledge the problem.

Active members might eventually become leaders in the social system, and these leaders need their own care and feeding. First comes the task of developing a process and criteria for determining good leadership candidates, together with recruiting people to fill roles that the social instance might need. These are volunteer positions, and although not everyone will be willing to do this officially, it is worth treating them as leaders and possibly rewarding them.

Finally, CMs need to develop their own knowledge and relationships as well, both in the social instance and beyond it. CMs need to join the conversations of their own groups, not necessarily acting as a knowledge expert, but perhaps by putting a familiar face before the members. Interfacing with other social instances with similar focus can help build those weak ties that bring in new blood. With the vibrant technological developments in social computing, CMs might also need to keep up with new tools, ideas, and approaches as they become available. This means learning from people, sites, books, and events focused on social computing. The study of community management is not yet a hard science or a common repeatable process, so the best opportunities for CMs are those in which they can learn from other CMs in online events or live events just for this kind of job.[7]

Topic and Activity Development

In addition to developing the relationships in the group, CMs must develop the topic. Not all social experience models are group oriented, so some degree of negotiation might be needed on the topic or goals for a social instance. Even individual bloggers often ask what their readers think they should focus on, to encourage that involvement. Over time, CMs might need to ask the group or expand the topic as the flow changes, and identify special interests or niches for a subset of membership.

Developing goals can lead to creating and working on activities or projects together, which requires some degree of project-management skills: defining project goals, identifying possible results,

---

[7] The number of events focused on social media and community management has experienced some explosive growth since 2005. Many commercial events take place in this sphere: larger ones such as the O'Reilly Web 2.0 Expos (www. web2expo.com) and the Community 2.0 event (community20.com), as well as smaller regional ones such as the Social Media Breakfast (www.socialmedia-breakfast.com/), held in a number of cities across North America and elsewhere.

scheduling people involvement, and setting targets and milestones. This can be fairly casual or can be formalized through a certified project management professional. For example, developing content for the social instance is one of the most common tasks. Members, CMs, or other roles can all provide content. However, to generate a regular flow of content, the CM might need to organize a simple publishing schedule to make sure that the other members have a steady stream of content to consume (see the sidebar "Stoking the Fires of Conversation").

In addition to content and activities is the culture that emerges out of each instance. Culture takes form through stories, images, lingo, and other cultural artifacts that the members repeatedly bring up or distribute to others. The CM's task is to capture and collect these, and help redistribute and reinforce the culture (described later in the section "Communications and Promotion").

Administrative Tasks

As with any project or activity, the CM frequently needs to measure and report on activities that the social group undertakes. This sort of administrative task can fall into different categories: traffic, structural, tasks, enablement, engagement, culture, and business. These and other administrative tasks define the specific governance policies and guidelines (beyond the high-level governance model that the CM might have chosen); the business rules for ratings, reputation, award, or other incentive systems; and the business operations, resource planning, and budgeting for the social instance.

On the surface, it appears that group-oriented social experiences focus more on policies and guidelines than individual ones. However, this is because group-oriented experiences generally also have governance systems that enable more people to contribute directly on an equal basis. This means that governance models, such as the representative, starfish, and swarm models, need to encourage more people to agree on a common cultural context. Therefore, the CM might need to establish guidelines on acceptable behavior in the experience. Most public-facing social experiences also develop acceptable usage guidelines and policies to create defensible criteria for handling issues and problem users.

Stoking the Fires of Conversation

Enticing conversation tends to be one of the CM's top tasks, particularly in social experiences in which members might not know each other directly. Many resources describe tips for better conversations in social media:[8]

- Point out posts from your members that might be conversation starters.

- Find the potential influencers in your system and invite them to engage in particular questions or discussions.

- Emphasize a short list of direct points that users can grasp quickly.

- Bring out debatable points, perhaps showing both sides of the debate.

- Look for compelling examples outside your own social environment and bring them to the attention of your social group. If you think a discussion, a blog, or content elsewhere on the Web is relevant to your own group, you should point it out, add a trackback or a link, contact the author, analyze the content, or add questions for your own group.

- Go off topic or offer a secondary place for off-topic conversations. Other conversations often pick up, adding dimension to your social group.

[8] Chris Brogan, *50 Ways to Take Your Blog to the Next Level*, ChrisBrogan.com (14 September 2008). This site has a useful list that is aimed at bloggers but applies to other social experiences as well. The Word of Mouth Marketing Association has a section called WOM 101 that also relates to this subject (see http://womma.org/wom101).

Similarly, points-based ratings or reputation systems might need situational business rules for how to distribute these points in a balanced manner, and to prevent users from unfairly creating advantageous situations for them—this is the act of *gaming* or cheating the system.

Finally, CMs might be responsible for budget and operations planning. These are the classic business issues of balancing costs for people resources, software applications, incentive programs, or marketing programs, and other factors of running a system for which someone eventually has to foot the bill.

Communications and Promotion

Communication is another large part of a CM's job. It starts with the basics of communicating content available in the social instance, either with other members or externally to draw them to the instance. When members visit the instance, the CM needs to show them where to find tips, guides, and training for using the social tool itself, to make it easier for users to accept and get involved in the instance.

If the social instance has evolved its own particular culture, part of the job is communicating and reinforcing these cultural values as acceptable and unacceptable behavior. Sharing stories, logos, phrases, terminology, and other cultural artifacts helps CMs shine the spotlight on other members, ongoing activities, and interesting recent interactions. The goal is to introduce these members and reinforce their actions or identity with others, as examples of good results or behavior. This provides opportunities to build relationships and essentially develop a path to a leadership role.

Content and culture provide the CM with ideas to talk about and share with external groups. Whether casually posting these ideas to other social environments or formally creating marketing tactics and programs, the goal is the same: to draw members from other social instances and ecosystems to your own. Formal methods include advertising or partnering with other social sites, or advertising on relevant non–social content sites. CMs also sometimes participate in shared results and anecdotes in external events to promote their social instance.

A CM might also consider having an event just for members. Social instance members might organize meetups and *birds-of-a-feather* sessions in conjunction with or separately from major conferences for their interest area, to increase the likelihood of meeting fellow members. Live events might seem contrary to the purpose of an online social group, but they work to support relationships on a different level—through direct personal and real-time interactions. The physical proximity can introduce new levels of understanding from actually hearing each other's voices, watching body language, and observing mannerisms. These physical aspects are often stripped from a social environment because of the limitations of the online medium. When people return from such live experiences, the bonds of benevolence usually hold even stronger.

Beyond shining the spotlight on activities, CMs might need to share success stories and anecdotes about productive member behavior and communicate the results of the activity in the social instance either to other members themselves or to the sponsors and stakeholders who support the social instance. The metrics collected as part of the administrative tasks express different sides to a social group. The industry view on measuring social computing and social media is not standardized. Depending on the social task, purpose, and organization, the important metrics can vary.

Business Development

Social environments in the public, cross-boundary, or third-party domains (see Chapter 6, "Social Ecosystems and Domains") are sometimes a way for companies to find new customers, develop new business opportunities, make money, or cover costs. Whatever the need, some common approaches arise for generating revenue:

- Charging a fee to members
- Selling items to members
- Brokering transactions between members
- Selling advertising space on an instance
- Scanning the membership for potential customers or business opportunities
- Selling products of member interactions (gathered knowledge, relationship structures, created artifacts, survey results, and so on) to others

Members' reactions to any of these processes can vary, depending on members' views of the terms under which they joined. Changing some aspect to generate revenue after the social environment has matured can be quite disastrous. For example, Facebook created the Beacon advertising system that tracked certain activities of its members in 40 participating Web sites and reported those activities to each member's set of friends. Civic groups such as MoveOn.org[9] petitioned Facebook to change the system to require that members be allowed to opt out of the system. However, Stefan Berteau of the Threat Research Group at Computer Associates discovered that even after the opt-out mechanism was instituted, the Beacon system continued to broadcast to the member's network of friends. Facebook's pursuit of business development essentially broke some of the trust that members had in the company.

In addition to finding ways to generate revenue, CMs might need to work with the sponsoring organization's marketing team, especially when the social instance involves customers. This means balancing the needs of the business against the welfare of the members, and advising the marketing team on what tactics might work for the membership. The task can include performing market analysis, collecting opinion or information from the social group, and devising marketing tactical actions that involve the members.

Summary

As described in the previous chapter, social leaders need to understand what encourages members to build their commitment and loyalty to a social experience. These activities typically fall on a job role that works across all the activity roles—the CM.

Whether they have full-time roles or do this part time, CMs face a variety of responsibilities and require numerous "soft" skills, traits, and behaviors. As more teams begin to work through online collaborative environments, these skills become a necessary element of employees and managers. Many organizations might not have official CMs; instead, they essentially spread these tasks among the leaders who participate in such environments. These skills and responsibilities can vary with the social experience and the involvement that

---

[9] In August 2008, a lawsuit was filed in California against Facebook and some of its business partners who participated in the Beacon system, such as Blockbuster, Zappos.com, Overstock.com, and others (http://blog.wired.com/ 27bstroke6/2008/08/facebook-beacon.html). At the time of writing, this had not yet been resolved in the courts.

sponsors expect. The next chapter looks at how CMs can measure the involvement and activity occurring in their social environments through different approaches.

10

Measuring Social Environments

Do consultants who are well connected to others online perform better than those who are not? Do projects involving people from different teams or departments of consultants really work better? How much increased business or revenue does that actually translate into?

These questions directly involve the relationships of people in business networks with the equation for success. The questions seek to discover new ways of improving productivity without changing the nature or products of the business.

Researchers from MIT Sloan School of Management and IBM[1] recently attempted to find these answers in a study of the online network relationships and communications of more than 2,600 consultants with any of the 400,000 employees in the same large company. By comparing the revenues that consultants generated by their billable hours against how they worked with others across their social network, the researchers were able to demonstrate that the topology of the network has a strong relationship to their work performance. For example, they found that just the size of a consultant's network did not translate to increased performance. However, those people who were well connected to managers did well: Knowing one additional manager increased their monthly revenue by $588. The explanation indicated that the managers were more likely to call in the consultant on higher-value projects. And having a weak connection to

---

[1] Lynn Wu, Ching-Yung Lin, Sinan Aral, and Erik Brynjolfsson, "Value of Social Network—A Large-Scale Analysis on Network Structure Impact to Financial Revenues of Information Technology Consultants," Winter Information Systems Conference, Salt Lake City, UT (February 2009). This paper is available at http://smallblue.research.ibm.com/publications/Utah-ValueOfSocialNetworks.

managers—by not knowing them well enough—led to a *decrease* of $98 a month.

This study points to wins for a particular group and the dollar value of building relationships through their online networks, but it is not a universal statement for all social systems. Still, it points out an important factor: Measuring social environments can lead to a better understanding of its contribution to a business.

What Can You Measure?

Unfortunately, although it might be possible to measure the visible or directly identifiable elements of social environments, such as how people are connected in business relationships, it is not as simple to measure other aspects of the system. To understand the significance, consider that the value of social systems—the *social capital*—takes three forms: *structural*, *relational*, and *cognitive*.[2] Structural social capital focuses on roles, networks, connections, and other subjects. Relational social capital focuses on the elements of trust, social norms (accepted behavior), reputation, and identification (social imagination). Cognitive social capital focuses on shared context and purpose, such as common language (imagery), values, shared environment, social experience, shared tasks, shared history (storytelling), and leadership.

A standardized universal approach still eludes us. Researchers at the World Bank concluded that one could measure the different aspects of social capital, but as *proxies* instead of actual valuations of social capital itself.[3] In other words, direct metrics in each of the types of social capital is not a direct conversion into dollars in every situation. Businesses also want to measure social environments for different reasons: They might have different types of measurement data

---

[2] Janine Nahapiet and Sumantra Ghoshal, "Social Capital, Intellectual Capital, and the Organizational Advantage," *Academy of Management Review* 23, no. 2 (1998): 243.

[3] Christian Grootaert and Thierry van Bastelaer, "Understanding and Measuring Social Capital: A Synthesis of Findings and Recommendations from the Social Capital Initiative" Social Capital Initiative working paper 24 (April 2001). Accessible at http://siteresources.worldbank.org/INTSOCIALCAPITAL/Resources/Social-Capital-Initiative-Working-Paper-Series/SCI-WPS-24.pdf.

available or are looking for different results, as you will see in the following examples.

Wikipedia and Google Knol enable a worldwide audience to gather knowledge socially. Some of their key metrics include the number of articles published on their sites, the number of contributors to these articles, and how actively they contribute. Large consulting organizations also keep track of knowledge. They can have intricate formal processes for collecting and packaging the knowledge they produce as assets, which they then measure in terms of how often their consultants reuse such knowledge assets and how much revenue or how many consulting deals are related to the asset. In both scenarios, a social group is involved in collecting and analyzing this information, and packaging it as accepted knowledge.

When projects appear on the research project crowdsourcing site InnoCentive, different members propose their competitive solutions to the project sponsors. InnoCentive can measure the average number of times users view a project, the number of project proposals fulfilled, the average bid per project, or even how long on average it takes for a solution to appear.[4]

On the social lending site Prosper.com, any member can lend money to others at specified interest rates.[5] Borrowers compete to find the lowest interest rate that they would like to pay, and lenders look to find the best return from their customers. The amounts could vary from less than $100 to tens of thousands of dollars. This process also reshapes money lending by enabling groups of members to pool their financial resources to lend to or borrow from others. This group orientation not only distributes the risk, but also creates a reinforcing network of peers to keep to the agreement. Both borrowers and lenders rate each other's transactions throughout the process. These metrics focus not only on the credit ratings of both parties, but also on how different categories of lending (such as home mortgage, auto, business, or personal loans) fare.

---

[4] Henry Chesborough, *Open Business Models: How to Thrive in the New Innovation Landscape* (Boston: Harvard Business School Press, December 2006).

[5] Prosper.com provides a detailed guide on how its social lending system works at www.prosper.com/welcome/how_it_works.aspx.

BzzAgent[6] and other social marketing sites offer programs to enlist enthusiasts and evangelists and to track how marketing messages offered by sponsors can spread through their network. The metrics include the key promoters per offering, the response to an offering, and the pattern of the spread.

Product support online communities from Apple to Ziff-Davis Media often combine the goals of developing further awareness of the company's offerings with developing a loyal base of customers. A host of metrics are possible: the number of responses each support request gets from the community, the average amount of time it takes to get a response, the number of new members to the community, the number of returning members, and the engagement of members in different marketing and loyalty offerings.

These examples are only a handful of social environments that are implementing different social tasks, but they already point out the bountiful variety of metrics involved. Some of these metrics rely on other metrics on different levels. They might also provide different information about the social environment, such as the count of knowledge or content within, the structure of relationships, the activity and health of the social group as a whole, or business value results.

It is easy to consider metrics and results when you have a lot of data, but how does one get this data? What are the processes or mechanisms for gathering this data? There's often more than one type of metric or a combination of metrics to examine. How do they relate to each other and what combinations really work?

And if social interactions and relationships produce the value of social environments, how do you know if a social group is really at a good point to produce results? This is a different dynamic than just collecting the data; it requires recognizing the right time to collect data.

The first step is recognizing the different types of metrics.

---

[6] BzzAgent supports online word-of-mouth marketing campaigns. See www.bzzagent.com/pages/Page.do?page=Why-Join-BzzAgent.

Dimensions of Measurement

Social-software metrics mean different things at different levels. For example, as an individual in an enterprise social community, I'd be interested in the network and type of relationships that I have with others, I'd want to track the items that I've contributed, and I'd want to know who finds my contributions useful. The community manager would be interested in looking at the aggregate results of all the members of the community. The ecosystem team that runs all these communities would be interested in the overall performance of the communities, and ways to compare how one is doing relative to another.

This introduces three common scopes for metrics: individual members and content items that I will metaphorically refer to as *leaves*; all the members or participants of a particular social instance, the entire *tree*; and all the members and participants in all social instances, in the same ecosystem or *forest*.

Individuals will be most interested in the metrics about themselves—the leaf metrics. Other users might be interested in a person's leaf metrics, but this triggers the question of which information should be private. Many social software users are getting comfortable with the idea of sharing some of their leaf metrics: the size of their social network, how frequently people read their posted content, or how others have rated their content. They see this as a way to encourage more people to interact with them, or to demonstrate their expertise or influence.

A community manager might also be interested in the leaves, especially when trying to identify influencers and their degree or form of influence. However, they are also subject to the rules of member privacy, depending on the agreed-upon terms and conditions of participating in the social environment.

The tree and forest levels describe aggregated behavior, although these are not necessarily just aggregations of people. You can have many levels of aggregations on top of each other, but I'll keep it simple here. Aggregating information often removes the personally identifying information about individual members, which makes it easier to access or share these metrics.

Types of Metrics

Each of these three views of a social environment's content also includes several different categories of metrics in which people might be interested. With so many metrics to choose from (see Table 10.1), it is easy to confuse which one is being discussed in ordinary conversation. Table 10.1 can act as a tool to declare the scope and type of metric, even if it is not an exhaustive list of possible choices in each of these categories.

TABLE 10.1   Metrics Categories Per Social Environment Scope

	Leaf Level (Each Person or Content Item)	Tree Level (Each Social Instance)	Forest Level (Each Ecosystem of Instances)
Traffic (behavioral)	Monthly Web page views, incoming Internet domains, incoming geolocation, monthly unique visitors, monthly repeat visitors, trackbacks, and average time spent on site	Monthly Web page views, incoming Internet domains, incoming geolocation, monthly unique visitors, monthly repeat visitors, and average time spent on site	Monthly Web page views, incoming Internet domains, incoming geolocation, monthly unique visitors, monthly repeat visitors, and average time spent on site
Structural (behavioral)	Connections (unidirectional or bidirectional), network size, social instances to which someone belongs, number of entries in the tag, and term frequency	Number of members, percentage of active and inactive members, and leadership roles created and filled	Number of social instances, and social instances per context model

TABLE 10.1   Metrics Categories Per Social Environment Scope

	Leaf Level (Each Person or Content Item)	Tree Level (Each Social Instance)	Forest Level (Each Ecosystem of Instances)
Tasks (behavioral and attitudinal)	Social tasks in which someone has participated, or content that he or she has created	Percentage of member task participation, percentage of task completion, success stories and outcomes from completed tasks, abandonment, content submissions, and postings	Social instances with a high degree of completions, and success stories about social instances
Commitment (behavioral and attitudinal)	Content-quality rating, content, content ranking on search engines, benevolence or competence reputation, number of recommendations or testimonials, and virtual currency	Rewards and awards given, number of members who acknowledge being enabled by the instance, and virtual currency transaction activity	Frequently reused context models, active social instances, virtual currency supply, and economy
Programs (behavioral and attitudinal)	Member programs or activities in which someone participates	Percentage of participation in engagement programs or activities, top active participants, and conversion per program	Percentage of participation in ecosystem-level engagement programs or activities, and conversion per program
Culture (attitudinal)	Cultural artifacts that a person has created or in which he or she is involved	Percentage of members who identify with the social instance's cultural artifacts, stories, storytellers, or age of artifacts	Percentage of members who identify with the ecosystem's artifacts, stories, age of artifacts, or number of instances with strong cultures

TABLE 10.1   Metrics Categories Per Social Environment Scope

	Leaf Level (Each Person or Content Item)	Tree Level (Each Social Instance)	Forest Level (Each Ecosystem of Instances)
Business (behavioral)	Purchase history, productivity in time saved, and face time with customers	Sales leads, revenue generated, top customers, sales trends, customer satisfaction, repeat-customer rate, support-cost savings, employee productivity in time saved, percent highly engaged employees, and improvement in employee time to productivity	Sales leads, revenue generated, top-selling instances, sales trends, customer satisfaction, repeat-customer rate, top customers, support-cost savings, employee productivity in time saved, percent highly engaged employees, and improvement in employee time to productivity

Traffic metrics are the most common type based on concepts that originate from measuring Web sites. These metrics tend to be the same in all three scopes, differing only by how many sources are aggregated in each scope.

Structural metrics describe the shape of networks and connections across them. This category is particularly interesting to the science of social-network analysis. By analyzing the structure of social networks, you can determine different information about relationships: the path or distance to a contact, the key liaison points or bottlenecks, or who in one's network is highly connected.

Task metrics are associated with the social tasks described in Chapter 4, "Social Tasks: Collaborating on Ideas," and Chapter 5, "Social Tasks: Creating and Managing Information." These metrics typically depend on the type of tasks, although generic tree- and forest-level metrics exist, such as the degree of participation and successful completion rate of tasks. In addition to these analytic measures, successful tasks and failures contribute to the social system's cultural history in the form of stories and heroes.

Engagement metrics relate to the reputation of individuals at the leaf level, or how influencers and leaders are rewarded for their activity at the tree and ecosystem levels. The analytic data of social gestures and exchanges, as described in Chapter 8, "Engaging and Encouraging Members," also falls into this category. The data can also be qualitative information, such as how aware members are of the culture and values of the social group.

Social environments that invite members to participate in particular programs or offerings introduce engagement metrics. These metrics are somewhat similar to task metrics but do not necessarily ask members to engage in a collaborative task. Instead, they tend to target members to participate individually. The similar metrics focus on how many members enroll in the offering, the degree of participation, and ways to successfully reach anticipated target numbers for each program or offering.

Cultural metrics describe the social group's cultural awareness, the variety of cultural artifacts they create and identify with, and the penetration of this culture across the group. Inevitably, other elements, such as tasks, programs, and structural relationships, also contribute to these metrics. For example, stories can surround any of these other metrics. As we will see later in this chapter, cultural metrics are also useful in describing a lifecycle to the growth and development of a social instance.

Metrics and Social Experiences

The metric categories in Table 10.1 describe what type of units to look for, but these units tend to differ across the different social experience models. For example, you could be looking for the same type of task or commitment metrics, but they could mean different things in different social experiences. Table 10.2 examines the differences between metrics in the various social-experience models.

These social-environment scopes also relate to how you define what constitutes an instance of a social environment or a collection of multiple instances. They distinguish the content items from the containers—and multiple levels of containers. From a metrics perspective, social-environment scopes identify different levels of

TABLE 10.2   Metrics per Social Experience at Different Scopes

	Leaf Level (Each Person or Content Item)	Tree Level (Each Social Instance)	Forest Level (Each Ecosystem of Instances)
Personal	Each individual's personalized view	Optional—different templates of personalized views can be different trees	Optional—if there are different templates, the forest of all these templates
Individual	Content within the individual's space	An individual space per person (such as one person's blog)	The collection of all individual spaces—for example, the collection of all blogs inside an enterprise
Social network	One person's network of members and interactions with them	Optional—the combined set of several people's social networks can be a tree	The combined set of all the individual social networks
Closed or visible groups	The individual members or content contributions of the group	Each group	The collection of all groups
Community	The individual members or content contributions of the community	Each community	The collection of all communities
Mass collaboration	Each content item a user contributes is a leaf—for example, one individual URL associated with a tag	A set of related content items—for example, the set of URL resources by the same tag	The collection of all sets of content items—for example, all the tags in a folksonomy

roughly comparable items. For example, you could roughly compare a member's published articles against others' articles at the leaf level in a group or other experience model, but you would not compare a single article (leaf) to an entire community (tree), or a single community (tree) to an entire ecosystem of communities (forest).

This is a common problem when, for example, someone sees a healthy community and asks why his or her entire ecosystem can't be exactly the same. It's a matter of scale and situation: Not all the communities in an ecosystem might have the same level of involvement, resource commitment, or support. It is also the same reason why you should not point to one or two successful communities in an ecosystem of many and judge the entire ecosystem to be healthy and successful. As the saying goes, this is comparing apples to oranges.

Measurement Mechanisms and Methods

Measuring aspects of social systems involves measuring both behavior and attitudes or opinions. These can be either quantitative or qualitative measurements, objective or subjective. Online environments can make this measurement both easier and complicated. Some social software builds in mechanisms to track structural behavioral data as part of each member or social instance; for example, LinkedIn keeps track of each member's number of connections and the size of the network. You can apply other tools, such as Google Analytics, to a Web site to gather site-traffic behavioral data.

Similarly, online tools for polling and surveys are particularly useful in measuring qualitative information of attitudes, awareness, and opinions. Let's take a closer look at these two methods for quantitative and qualitative measurement to understand how they apply to the different types of metrics identified earlier.

Quantitative Analytic Measurement Mechanisms

Quantitative tools for Web site measurement have existed for years and have easily transferred to social sites. As mentioned before, Google Analytics is available to anyone on the public-facing Internet domain for free. Other tools, from companies such as Omniture and WebTrends, can work in several different domains, from public-facing domains to the enterprise domain. These quantitative tools can track a wide range of metrics in Table 10.1, except for cultural and commitment metrics, which are primarily qualitative measures.

Traffic metrics, such as Web page views and site-unique visitors, are the most common example of analytic metrics. Many sites report the size of their community in terms of the average number of unique visitors they receive each month, regardless of how many times each visitor might actually come to that site that month.

Structural metrics describe the connections or associations between entities, such as the number of members who belong to an instance, the connections a member has to others, or the size of the network that a member can reach. The leaf-level interpretation of connections can be either the number of relationships that a member has formed with others or the number of links to a document. The latter is famously involved in Google's Pagerank algorithm but can also be the number of entries mapped to a social tag (how often that tag is connected to a resource). Relationships to a person can be bidirectional (both parties agree to form the bond) or unidirectional (many people follow an individual's activity).

Tasks that can be broken down into steps or measured in terms of successful completions can be analytic even if the output itself is qualitative. The quantitative measure is in terms of member participation in these tasks. Similarly, member participation in any kind of program aimed at a social instance or ecosystem (such as promotion, content submission, member-to-member engagement, rewards, and enablement programs) can be set up in terms of quantitative measures. Reputation or quality metrics can be either objective measures, such as a numeric scoring system, or subjective measures, such as recommendations, testimonials, and reviews.

Qualitative Measurement through Surveys and Interviews

Trying to learn qualitative information about a social instance is less of a science and more of an art in identifying attitudes and opinions. Certain tools can be helpful, especially when formalized through surveys, but it is also beneficial to gather this information through direct dialogue, interviews, and focus groups. These skills are specific to user-experience design and user testing, and are often used in product testing. Online survey tools from SurveyMonkey and

Vovici[7] make the process of creating and conducting these surveys simple and often affordable. However, knowing how to use these tools is one thing—knowing what to ask people in a survey is a whole different consideration.

Qualitative questions are often a step of discovery, asking for opinions on current items or unforeseen alternative options. Users consider opinion gathering useful if the community managers (CMs) or sponsors can show some action or outcome from these opinions. They want to know that their opinion will matter; therefore, a survey must offer information on what actions will follow if users take the time to complete it.

Users might receive a constant barrage of surveys and polls just because they use the Internet, and this barrage of demands doesn't help when trying to study one's own social instance. Katrina Lerman and Manila Austin of Communispace suggest[8] balancing the mechanisms for studying a community almost equally among surveys, dialogues, and focus groups.

Focus groups, dialogues, and interviews provide a different approach to collecting qualitative information. The difficult part is finding appropriate representatives for these groups. Reaching out to leaders in a social experience can give a wide and deep view, but this also collects the opinion of the more active members of an instance, which the newer and less active members might not share. The purpose of interviews is to go beyond preset questions (as in a survey); follow trains of thought, arguments, and highlights; and then investigate these issues more deeply with the interviewees.

The final approach is to gather data from the flow of information in the social group: scan the contributions from members over time, collect opinions and issues, and analyze them. This task is less labor-intensive if it is part of the CM's monthly or regular operations and analysis.

---

[7] SurveyMonkey is a low-cost Web tool for creating, delivering, and managing online surveys at www.surveymonkey.com/. Vovici provides a similar commercial service for surveys on the Internet or within a company at www.vovici.com/index.aspx.

[8] Katrina Lerman and Manila Austin, *Creating a Culture of Participation*, Brief Report, Communispace (2007). Accessible at www.communispace.com/research/abstract/?Type=All%20About%20Communities&Id=33.

Analyzing qualitative answers means finding commonalities across interviewees, categorizing or tagging these commonalities, and marking frequency. This helps identify hot spots and alludes to priorities for which topic to address first. You might also consider the reputation of the interviewees as a form of ranking, if this is an important consideration.

Summary

Metrics in social systems involve a number of dimensions: individuals versus social instances and ecosystems, quantitative versus qualitative measures, behavior versus attitudes, and metrics collected for different reasons. The best guide is to choose metrics based on what matters for the social instance and the context model. Focus on task achievement, member engagement and alignment to the sponsor, or stronger social ties and culture.

Metrics serve to support the organization's strategy and goals. Therefore, social computing systems exist not simply as another communication channel, but as specific pieces that are necessary to execute business strategy. This requires the right application of social systems to serve the overall strategy.

11

Social Computing Value

Social computing is a general methodology that applies human interests, ingenuity, and analysis to a range of business problems that are not practical or possible to solve with raw machine computational power. The element of "computation" here is the process of how people discover, consider, interpret, and communicate ideas through various means. These are not formulaic processes; each person brings his or her own unique history, expertise, and personality when working on the problem. This element of creativity separates social computing from mathematical and analytical models possible through software code and algorithms. Yet social computing still requires a software-assisted medium that works through online environments to allow people to interact across distances. It is particularly helpful when working across multiple organizational departments, companies, or job roles. It can apply to different scenarios within a single enterprise, between a business and its customers, between shareholders and the public directly, or even when engaging customers at other popular online venues.

It is considered *social* because the information can be segmented, shared, distributed, or recombined across the efforts of many individuals. For social computing to work, most often the people involved need to see each other's contributions. In other cases, this information is aggregated from many individual sources into larger or more complex packages to deliver to others. This is also social because of the relationships and trust bonds that form between people while working on such problems.

Successful social computing environments can even help users transcend the immediate task and develop long-lasting working relationships. It opens participants' minds to new ideas, new possibilities, and sometimes even new opportunities through their interactions. CEOs point to this deeper and wider level of collaboration as a key to business innovation. Social computing can also counteract the sense of isolation among an increasingly distributed or telecommuting workforce.

The 50-plus examples in this book highlight different aspects of how organizations have implemented social computing to solve particular business needs. These aspects describe how people gather together, lead others, work on tasks, develop a shared purpose and culture, and commit to participate. They also describe what it takes to guide this participation, develop the focus, and measure activity.

As with any method, specific repeatable techniques can be applied to different scenarios. People participate within defined structures and steps. However, social environments are also fluid entities that often depend on the attitudes, preferences, and personalities of the participants. Much depends upon the maturation of the social group as a whole.

Applying social computing techniques involves its own particular style of leadership, enablement, and guidance. Unlike traditional teams in hierarchical organizations that come under the direction of people managers, social computing takes a new brand of social *community* managers and uses different methods to engage participation in work tasks.

Defining the Structure of a Social Environment

Implementing social computing methods requires a number of initial steps to plan or create the structure of the social environment. This involves refining the choices for the social experience, the leadership model, the social tasks, the grouping, and the domain desired for the social environment.

Choosing a Social Experience

Working in any online social computing environment places a person into one of several models of *social experiences*. These experiences describe how people are grouped together in a collaborative setting. This differs from a personal experience, such as shopping at fashion retailer Coach's online store, where each customer's purchase is entirely isolated from others', without any feedback between customers about products.

Each experience identifies whether the environment revolves around the interests of a person, a particular group, or a shared topic. Although every environment is social—some level of interaction occurs between people—each experience model defines an approach to the directness of interaction: who can provide input, where the output goes and what form it takes, and who generally has control of the experience. Each social experience model can simultaneously provide benefits to owners, members, and sponsors in different ways.

For example, last.fm implements the mass collaboration experience that allows each user to see what others recommend for similar music. At the same time, it engages its fans to continue listening as return customers for the business. Slideshare allows an individual experience in which users can share their presentations online with others. LinkedIn engages users to invite their business contacts into a social network experience, which adds more people into the overall system to help others to discover new contacts, increasing the overall value of this social Web site.

Immediate and virtual teams can use IBM Lotus Quickr to interact with each other across an organization in a single online environment reserved for this closed workgroup experience. The Music Genome Project, on the other hand, enlists experts into a visible workgroup experience to share their results with customers on Pandora Internet radio. SAP Developer Network engages a wide range of customers across many industries and locations into an online community experience to discuss and share their expertise to solve complex problems, while at the same time encouraging greater use of SAP products.

Setting a Social Leadership Model

The owners of these social environments can choose particular approaches for how they create and guide the direction of content in various forms of social leadership models. Each model describes the approach of assigning leaders the rights of other users to participate and contribute to the shared experience (or allowing leaders to emerge from the membership of the social environment), and determining who is involved in the decisions for the direction of the social environment.

The most basic is the centralized model of leadership, in which a single person, team, or organizational representative has ownership of the social environment. For example, sites such as Businessweek.com and CNN.com might allow members to submit comments and feedback for others to see, but the articles and direction of the content fall within the control of editorial teams of each organization. Most individual blogs on the Web are a similarly centralized model: Only the blog owner decides the content, participation, and direction for the blog. In contrast, some blogs, such as BoingBoing.net, are shared across a group of people, with each individual focusing on his or her interests and topics under the common banner. This delegated model spreads the leadership across several individuals or groups to manage the direction. *Scientific American* magazine uses a similar technique to delegate questions to experts with different areas of scientific expertise.

Larger groups of people, such as the IEEE Computer Society, might choose a representative model, in which each local chapter and special interest group can elect or decide upon its own leaders. This contrasts with the entirely volunteer or temporary leadership in starfish leadership models evident in software development projects from the Apache Foundation or in Alcoholics Anonymous, for example. At the other extreme is the swarm leadership model, in which everyone plays a part in the purely democratic decision-making process; true leadership depends on indirect influence or on the commonality of interests.

The social experience model can limit the available choices of leadership models. Social networks and individual experiences typically use centralized or delegated models in which ownership and leadership remains within a small group of individuals. Closed and visible groups can use centralized, delegated, representative, or starfish leadership models to decide their direction and participation. Community experiences might have delegated leadership but more typically involve representative or starfish models. A mass collaboration relies on the temporary, volunteer leadership of a starfish or the distributed democratic process of a swarm.

Defining a Social Task

Both social experience and leadership models apply to different types of tasks designed for social groups. A social task directs members to collectively engage and interact in steps of a collaborative process to produce some end result. Each task can benefit some subset of the membership, the entire membership, the sponsors, or even other groups and causes. In addition, the aggregation of the work across the group can occur in several different approaches: independent outcomes aggregated into a single collective value, autonomous work attributable to each member working separately from others, consensus gathering across the group, deliberation and debate of multiple possible ideas, and combative approaches to get to the best choice of all the ideas.

The two dozen examples of organizations in Chapters 4, "Social Tasks: Collaborating on Ideas," and 5, "Social Tasks: Creating and Managing Information," describe a number of distinctly separate social tasks. For example, IBM's InnovationJam and Dell's Ideastorm are social brainstorming projects to engage many individuals to submit, deliberate on, and choose good ideas for implementation into these companies' research or product-development efforts. Prediction markets, such as electronics retailer BestBuy's TagTrade system, enable members to price their ideas of value for a given item, collectively resulting in a final market price.

BurdaStyle's approach of allowing its members to create new sewing pattern designs after choosing and applying templates (crowdsourcing by template) encourages customers to promote their own designs and consider new choices, while helping the company sell more products. The Amazon Web Services Mechanical Turk project enables sponsors to divide analysis work across a crowd to find a collective answer to problems through a process of distributed human computation. InnoCentive's approach, on the other hand, enables different individuals or teams to bid on research projects in exchange for a financial bounty. Open source software development focuses on drawing potential workers from anywhere who share an interest in the vision of the project, and then coordinating their work as a social group.

BranchIt Software and IBM Lotus Atlas for Connections enable members of a social group to map their network of relationships across a larger group and find connection paths to others. Social tools such as Dopplr and Brightkite can also enable people either to find other members from their group who are physically nearby or to discover others with similar interest in their geographical area.

Vendors such as PowerReviews, BazaarVoice, and Amazon.com enable users to collect and share reviews about products or items, an excellent way to gather social wisdom and views that help encourage or focus further product purchases. In contrast to sharing "to all customers," other social tasks focus on directly recommending content or products to people in your social group, such as when using the Flock browser to share pictures and Web links with peers. Some systems, such as Netflix and last.fm, apply software processes to derive automated recommendations to share with others.

Aside from recommendations, users can share and collaborate on a number of social tasks, in content and collections. Retailer Amazon.com's online store enables users to create wish lists or collections of products to share with their peers and friends. Sites such as Wikipedia and Google Knol task groups of people to directly create or edit knowledge on a wide range of subjects, while Mahalo applies this group knowledge to provide answers from its search engine. Zoominfo, on the other hand, derives content from many sources to provide information about people and connect them in social networks.

Social bookmarking and tagging on sites such as del.icio.us, Reddit, Stumbleupon, or Dogear enable users to categorize and identify information as a collective view to understand how ideas relate to one another. Many Web sites, such as MarketWatch.com, also guide users toward new information based on such social activities as the most-read or most-commented articles in their daily news that bring out what interests people the most. Yahoo! Answers, on the other hand, helps users ask, filter, and navigate to direct questions and answers among the social population.

Grouping Experiences and Identifying the Audience Domain

Organizations also find value in grouping together different social environments, each pursuing its own agenda. Wordpress, for example, provides an entire ecosystem of blogs to many individuals and groups, each working for its own goals and direction while still using essentially the same software system. GoingOn, on the other hand, combines multiple social software tools into packaged solutions for schools and other educational institutions, as well as tools for supporting live conference events as online social environments. These combinations either help bring together many people toward a general higher purpose (such as blogging) or allow a single membership of users to interact in different social tasks for the same overall goal.

Defining where an audience comes from—the social domain—can help unify the membership or introduce radically different cultures into one environment. Intel, GE, and the U.S. Air Force all provide online social environments to enable their employees to interact in a private manner within the context of their company. Verizon Wireless and SAP Developer Network public communities encourage customers to raise and address technical problems they might have in common, essentially providing another product support channel for the parent organizations. General Motors and Ernst & Young both take part in well-known third-party public social sites where their customers and interested parties already are participating, to draw them into their marketing or recruiting efforts. IBM's LotusLive social computing service allows organizations to conduct private sessions and events directly between employees and customers, such as during sales calls, executive presentations, and complex support sessions.

Social domains introduce differential concerns for governance policies. Working in an employee-only environment requires different governing principles than when involving a mixed audience of customers and employees. Similarly, people from these different audiences bring their own work cultures, and working in a mixed environment requires some normalization and agreement on social behaviors and norms.

Cultural Forces Shaping Social Environments

The cultural differences in how people work are major factors when working with or leading people in social environments that typically come from different teams, organization units, companies, or roles. Therefore, understanding cultural differences among social groups can be significant when seeking productivity.

Culture, in this context, exists within the social environment itself instead of in the geopolitical origins of members. Although these national cultures certainly have an effect on how a person works, each social group can develop its own private culture. This exists outside online environments, too: You can be a citizen of the United States while still having distinct preferences for or against the chrome-and-leather motorcycle culture of Harley-Davidson fans.

Distinctive artifacts of culture can become apparent through the interactions of members. Shared visual and aural imagery—such as the artwork, the clothing style, and even the very sound associated with the Harley-Davidson motorcycle culture—helps members identify each other, in addition to stating their tastes and product preferences. The use of all caps in text messages is another such cultural element, one fairly universally abhorred in e-mail and online interactions. Storytelling creates a shared cultural history in a social group, identifying values or describing good or unacceptable behaviors.

For any artifact to become part of the culture, the leaders and members must retransmit and validate the ideas. The development of cultural artifacts and the level of acceptance of these artifacts indicate how close alignment is among the members.

Commitment to a social environment is a combination of each member's alignment with the culture, acceptance of the vision or goals imagined for the group, and engagement with the activities of the social group. It is possible to view commitment in social environments in terms of distinct levels. These range from members who are trying to get accustomed to working with others in an online environment, to the top members who selflessly work for the social group in mentoring and leading (see Figure 8.1 from Chapter 8, "Engaging and Encouraging Members").

Realizing value in social computing activities hinges on getting members to participate. Members do not participate simply because they are told to do so; they need encouragement and social development, from other members and often from a central leadership role of a community manager.

Community managers focus on guiding members to increase their participation in the goals of the social environment. This can apply to any type of social experience. Even without a formal title, these tasks typically fall upon the leaders of the environment. Community managers can introduce programs such as membership rewards, evangelist recognition, and mentoring to newer members, to encourage commitment at different levels.

The key value of community managers lies in being an advocate and intermediary between the members and the sponsors. They help move the work toward increased productivity by guiding individuals, focusing activities, and generally trying to herd cats—trying to get many people with individual motivations to move in a common direction. Community managers also help relate the activity in the social environment directly to the business activities and strategy of the sponsoring organization.

Social Computing and Business Strategy

Social computing methods that apply in business situations require ideation, review, and decision making by a group of people. Social tasks can produce results when given the right context and level of support, but they need to work within the larger context of the processes and structure of the sponsoring organization.

These methods are becoming common in marketing or social media activities: communicating ideas to people, helping spread the word, and collecting and sharing views. Such efforts are evident in a number of the examples from Slideshare, blogging, and BoingBoing.net, to the public interactions of Ernst & Young and General Motors. Sales processes frequently benefit from other social tasks for companies, such as Amazon.com, BurdaStyle, Netflix, last.fm, and Pandora. These organizations provide recommendations and guide customers to other products and options that might interest them, thereby increasing the possibilities of return or additional sales. Verizon Wireless and SAP Developer Network introduces new methods to support customers through the combined collective wisdom of employees and other customers. IBM's InnovationJam, InnoCentive's crowdsourcing methods, and the Apache Foundation's open source software-development efforts show social computing methods that support research and development activities through brainstorming and shaping ideas and goals, or by outsourcing entire projects.

Social computing facilitates new strategies that change how businesses can apply the collective efforts of many individuals to solve problems and contribute to the success of the organization. Understanding the dynamics of how these methods work is both a science and an art. This is not spurred solely by the use of software technology; it is the change in how businesses see themselves partnering with those all around them, to develop strategic gains in an increasing globally interdependent business climate. This interdependency will likely continue as emerging markets introduce new opportunities and competition, and as new generations of employees who have grown up in a world full of people and computer networks bring their skills in social computing to the workplace.

In the future, the skills of working in online social environments might become an increasingly common part of every job. A number of organizations today are already moving ahead by incorporating social computing into their strategies, giving them an extra edge by driving collaboration and productivity across employees, partners, customers, the public, and the entire sphere of people around them.

INDEX

UL Wharton School Publishing

In the face of accelerating turbulence and change, business leaders and policy makers need new ways of thinking to sustain performance and growth.

Wharton School Publishing offers a trusted source for stimulating ideas from thought leaders who provide new mental models to address changes in strategy, management, and finance. We seek out authors from diverse disciplines with a profound understanding of change and its implications. We offer books and tools that help executives respond to the challenge of change.

Every book and management tool we publish meets quality standards set by The Wharton School of the University of Pennsylvania. Each title is reviewed by the Wharton School Publishing Editorial Board before being given Wharton's seal of approval. This ensures that Wharton publications are timely, relevant, important, conceptually sound or empirically based, and implementable.

To fit our readers' learning preferences, Wharton publications are available in multiple formats, including books, audio, and electronic.

To find out more about our books and management tools, visit us at whartonsp.com and Wharton's executive education site, exceed.wharton.upenn.edu.